UNVEILING VIT

A New Life Emerging From Chronic Fatigue

Katie MacLarnon

Amazon KDP

Katie MacLarnon

Copyright © 2025 Katie MacLarnon

All rights reserved

No part of this book may be reproduced, or stored in a retrieval system, or transmitted in any form or by any means, electronic, mechanical, photocopying, recording, or otherwise, without express written permission of the publisher.

ISBN-13: 9798851513497

Cover design by: Jason Blackeye

First publication in 1988 under the title
M.E and Me by Susan Abrahams Limited
Second publication in 2011 under the title
Chronic Fatigue, Leaving M.E behind
by Katie MacLarnon LULU publishing

Dedication

To my late mum and dad, Sue, Alistair and Ian

Throughout the long afternoons, my head tilted towards the window, dark gloomy clouds whispered by. The weather seemed almost insignificant, unable as I was to experience cold winter winds or the soft patter of evening drizzle. One day rolled into the next with little to look forward to. Would the following day prove to be a little better or had I to experience the same dismal routine? It was impossible to know.

CONTENTS

Title Page	
Copyright	2
Dedication	3
Epigraph	4
Contents	5
Acknowledgements	7
Preface	8
PART ONE	11
Chapter One	13
Chapter Two	19
Chapter Three	27
Chapter Four	39
Chapter Five	53
Chapter Six	65
Chapter Seven	81
Chapter Eight	89
Chapter Nine	97
Epilogue One	103
PART TWO	109
Chapter Ten	111
Chapter Eleven	115
Chapter Twelve	119
Chapter Thirteen	121
Chapter Fourteen	125
Chapter Fifteen	129
Chapter Sixteen	133
Chapter Seventeen	139
Chapter Eighteen	145

Chapter Nineteen	149
Chapter Twenty	153
Chapter Twenty - One	157
Chapter Twenty - Two	161
Chapter Twenty - Three	163
Chapter Twenty - Four	167
Chapter Twenty - Five	173
Chapter Twenty - Six	185
Chapter Twenty - Seven	195
Chapter Twenty - Eight	207
Chapter Twenty - Nine	211
Epilogue Two	215
PART THREE	219
Chapter Thirty	221
Chapter Thirty - One	227
Chapter Thirty - Two	231
Chapter Thirty - Three	237
Chapter Thirty - Four	247
Chapter Thirty - Five	253
Chapter Thirty - Six	261
Chapter Thirty – Seven	265
Chapter Thirty - Eight	269
Epilogue Three	279
About The Author	281

ACKNOWLEDGEMENTS

To my late mum and dad who sadly did not see me regain my health and the achievements I've made, and to them both for all the help and support a daughter could ever want, their enduring patience and persistent hope.

To Sue, Alistair and Ian for always being there with great understanding and caring concern for their little sister.

To Kim without whom I doubt I would be here today, for his persistence in guiding me and supporting me throughout some of the hardest times in my life.

To Chris for taking the time to help me from afar and without whom I'm certain my recovery process would have been slower. I felt very lucky and privileged to have been one of his patients, using his complex effective treatments.

To Clive whose thoughtful patience, understanding and determination to help me become well again gave me the hope and encouragement I needed.

To my closest friends especially Annemarie, Sally and Dick who have encouraged me, given me strength and made me laugh!

PREFACE

The following is a very personal account of how I have struggled to pull through a very debilitating, misunderstood illness. As of July 2025, there are an estimated 404,000 cases of M.E/CFS Myalgic Encephalomyelitis or Chronic Fatigue Syndrome in the UK, This figure doesn't allow for people who suffer with Long Covid who will also have M.E. This brings the figure to an estimated 1 million in the UK, approximately 17-24 million cases of M.E worldwide. My story recounts the physical as well as the psychological challenges that I encountered, the effect on family life, progress, and setbacks. Learning of various methods to improve my condition, whether by orthodox or complementary medicine. Keeping hold of an enormous self-belief that one day I would be well again.

There are three parts to my story. Part One focuses on the first 18 months, with detailed descriptions of my medical difficulties, at times they may seem a little repetitive, but please bear with me as this was, is, unfortunately the nature of chronic fatigue. Also, bear in mind that I was still extremely unwell writing this section, it was a tremendous challenge particularly mentally, sometimes just to put sentences together. Now, as I read it back several years later, I felt it important not to edit this.

In Part Two and Part Three, the style of writing

differs, becoming more relaxed and less detailed on persistent medical difficulties the more well and able I became.

It has been beneficial, cathartic for me as an individual to express my feelings on paper. I hope that others will read this with no interest in chronic fatigue but find it an inspiring story. However, I would like to think other M.E sufferers who may read this might find it useful to share with others, so that they can have a better understanding of their illness. It is so often exceedingly difficult for others to fully appreciate unless they are a full time carer, or have consistent contact with a loved one with M.E. New effective therapies are now available that were unheard of during the early years I was unwell. Some of the health information and thoughts behind the illness from Part One are now outdated, written early in 1988.

Determination and continued, if sometimes difficult to believe in optimism, can and does go a long way to helping, qualities attributed to I think almost anyone with M.E.

My childhood and adolescent years were filled with incredibly good health, apart from a persistent neck injury. At age 21 my life changed forever, devastated by the long-term severe effects of M.E .....

Katie MacLarnon

PART ONE

Katie MacLarnon

CHAPTER ONE

In December 1986, I noticed I was becoming excessively tired after a day's work, with a loss of appetite for some time. It was not until a game of squash that I realised that something was wrong; after each game, I had to have a long period of rest. Subsequently, I thought I was coming down with 'flu. Over Christmas, my glands became swollen, my throat and tonsils inflamed, a general feeling of malaise continued into the New Year. Despite this, I continued with my twenty-first birthday party that had been planned for a while. Although feeling unwell throughout, I managed to entertain forty-five friends and colleagues until the small hours of the morning. The following week, the result of a blood test confirmed the suspicion of my GP that I might have glandular fever. Although I knew that in previous years friends of mine had taken a few weeks to recover, I had no idea what lay in store for me.

After three weeks away from work, I tried going back for a couple of hours twice a week. This was mentally and physically exhausting; my legs could no longer hold me up and on returning home, I had to spend the rest of the day in bed.

It was at this time that my parents had planned a holiday in New Zealand to visit my sister and their first grandchild whom they had never seen. They were on the verge of postponing their trip, but I managed to persuade them that I would be all right as I had two elder brothers to look after me. I was sure that I would be well again soon. After many discussions concerning my health, my parents continued apprehensively with their plans and left for New Zealand.

While they were away, with more time off work, I spent the majority of the day resting with short trips to the local shops by car for bare necessities. As each day passed, it became more and more difficult to walk around the house; my knees weak and painful on standing or walking more than about fifty meters at a time. I began to cling on to the furniture to get around the rooms as my knees were too painful to keep them straight when walking.

During that month I had days when I became very upset; worrying about the pain I was getting and because it seemed to get worse, not better. The medical reason for this was that it was just part of the illness, I had no reason to doubt this. I felt guilty about spending so much time away from work although my employer was very understanding. After continuously keeping in touch with my parents during the month they were away, they returned home expecting to find me much better than I was.

By the beginning of April, my symptoms seemed to be improving but I still had discomfort in my legs, particularly in my knees, so I visited a physiotherapist whom I had seen before for a previous injury. At first,

I found infrared heat beneficial along with some very gentle exercise; my walking seemed to be improving, although I could still only walk about 100 meters without feeling pain and weakness. Because of the duration of the illness, my GP thought it best for me to see a virologist just to check that things were all ok. I had a long, pleasant discussion with him with the outcome that things would get better soon.

The weather by now had improved, I spent many days in the garden sunbathing. This was all I was fit for; after walking downstairs from my room out into the garden I needed to rest. Two weeks later, I started to get severe headaches. Still feeling weak, I fainted after having a shower. That afternoon, I was admitted to the Churchill Hospital in Oxford for observation.

My short stay consisted of further blood tests and more pills for the pain in my leg muscles and headaches. Vomiting, and accompanied by the feeling that I had been drugged, my mind spinning, unable to concentrate on anything, I felt sleepy all the time. Exhausted, and apart from managing the three or four paces to the basin in my hospital room, I spent the long weekend confined to bed.

It was at this time that I began to have problems with my vision. With consistent headaches and poor concentration, I found it impossible to watch television, read or listen to the radio. I wanted to be on my own, in peace, and just wished the symptoms would disappear. For the doctors, they had a patient who spent most of her time in tears for no apparent reason; I felt miserable all the time and, as I had not encountered long-term illness before, felt that I had been ill long enough. I just wanted to be better and back home in surroundings I knew. After four unhappy days, they let me go home, although they would have preferred that I stay in a few more days. I left the ward in a wheelchair and, on returning home, had to be carried up to my room.

Over the next three weeks, my symptoms deteriorated. My hair began to fall out. I still felt as if I had 'flu all the time. The pain in my knees was so bad that apart from struggling to the bathroom when necessary, I confined myself to bed. I had to. Every time I got up, the pain just got worse. Getting out of bed was soon an impossibility. I spent almost every day crying; this exhausted me even more but I found it was the only way to express my feelings of anger and frustration for being in this condition.

My family were very supportive, but it was impossible for them to understand what I was going through and why I spent so much of my time crying. I felt so alone. Still unable to watch television, I spent most of the day thinking of what I had been through during the past six months, the pain I had had to endure and worst of all seeing no end to it.

I was very keen on sport and had excelled in all areas throughout my school years, athletics, tennis, hockey and gymnastics. I was always a member of the school teams, often captain of them. After a neck injury at the age of fourteen, I often had to opt out of some of the sporting activities much to my dismay as I was always very competitive. After leaving school I'd managed to continue playing squash, without sounding too immodest, I felt I was a young intelligent athletic individual who had always enjoyed life and who had always made the most of any opportunities that arose. Now, alone in my room, I missed the company of my friends; the routine of getting up and going to work every day; I rarely wanted visitors as I felt too tired to talk to them and felt I had nothing to say. After all, I hadn't done anything to talk about. Although trying very hard to be cheerful and optimistic, most of my conversations consisted of the pain I had been through and how miserable I had been. I was becoming a very quiet, depressive individual who shut herself away from the rest of the world. The Katie I knew with the lively personality was disappearing, it frightened me.

My dad, a doctor, was I think, particularly distressed at seeing me like this. He would come home from a hard day's work at the hospital to find another patient waiting for him. There was nothing he could do to help me. The helplessness, that close friends and particularly my family suffered was immensely difficult. There were many times, when I felt they suffered as much as me, longing to help in any way they could but unable to do so. Ironically, at this time, when friends and doctors told me it could not be much longer until I was better, it was more of a hindrance than a help.

Throughout the six months, as the weeks went by, my condition just seemed to deteriorate; I had good days when I thought I was making progress at last, but the bad days always seemed much worse, and got worse as time went on. I do not recall ever thinking there was anything else wrong with me; I just knew the virus was still there. There were days when I thought I'd had enough; I couldn't take any more. It seemed as though my entire world had collapsed. I began to understand the contemplation of suicide that some people go through; only for a few seconds, but something I would normally never have considered with my positive attitude for life. I don't know what I would have done if I had known I would be in this same position a year later.

CHAPTER TWO

It had been an enormous help to have a dad as a doctor, who could chase up some of his colleagues and keep on doing so until they come up with any potential suggestions to help. Although I am enormously grateful for my dad's help, as an adult I wanted to do things for myself. However, as time progressed, I became angrier about having to wait so long to try any treatment, just as any patient does for any illness they have to suffer from.

By the beginning of June, after a few helpful words from my dad to his colleagues, I was re-admitted to the Churchill Hospital for a week's treatment with an antiviral drug Acyclovir administered intravenously. This was no definite cure; I knew that. The doctors could not promise me anything, but they had found that it had previously helped in some patients. I was being offered this treatment as further blood tests had shown that I still had the virus present in my blood stream. I had been very fortunate to be offered that treatment as it was very expensive, not everyone had the chance to try it.

Although I should have been pleased that at last someone was trying to help me, I again spent the majority of my stay crying. I was becoming quite depressed. I felt sorry for the staff that had to put up with this miserable patient; for the first two days my almost hysterical crying could be heard quite a long way down the corridor. It was so stupid making such a fuss, but I seemed to be locked into a depressive mood, I couldn't snap out of it. The doctors were concerned about my behaviour; they thought it likely that there was something else worrying me that I hadn't mentioned. I knew that this wasn't the case, so did my parents. They knew that I was just upset because of the condition I was in, after all, they had had to live with me for the previous seven months; they knew how upsetting it must be for me to deal with the persistent pain and fatigue. However, I agreed, very apprehensively, to the doctor's suggestion that I should see a psychiatrist. It did concern me though; did they think I was mad? I'd never encountered psychiatric help before, this decision for me, was a very cautious one, however, I knew I couldn't continue in the state I was in for much longer. I think that deep down I needed to talk to someone, I desperately needed someone outside my family to understand me, to understand the misery I felt and could not always explain.

To spend the following six weeks with Dr A as an outpatient proved to be one of the best decisions I had made throughout my illness so far. After four days of the Acyclovir, I at last began to show some signs of improvement. The 'flu-like symptoms had departed from my body; the severe headaches had gone; and with great care I took my first steps ... For the first time in weeks, I could now stand at the basin and brush my teeth without the fear of falling at any slight attempt to keep my knees straight. It was as though my inner body had been spring-cleaned. My complexion was clearer, the sparkle had returned to my eyes. I knew this was the beginning and that I had turned the corner at last.

Over the next two days, I managed to walk the 15 meters down the corridor to the toilet instead of using the commode in my room. The pleasure of being able to do this small task was immense and the long lost smile returned to my weary but delighted face.

Something that still concerned me was my weight; I have a petite figure and am only five feet one inch tall and usually weigh seven stones; I was now exactly six stones and with my legs so thin and my face gaunt, I avoided any contact with mirrors. The doctors had given me permission to go home in the afternoon between the two and ten o'clock intravenous drip. I tried this on four occasions but found it far too exhausting. On the eighth day, I walked, at a very sedate pace out of the hospital, smiling. The small exertion of leaving my hospital room and then back into my own bedroom was so tiring that I spent the rest of the day in bed.

Over the next two weeks, I found everyday tasks, such as washing my hair, very arduous and even taking the quickest of showers took more strength out of me. (I could not take a bath, the water surrounding my legs gave me terrible cramp.) I had to rest for literally hours after even the slightest activity. This was something I had to get used to.

During this time, I began my visits to see Dr A at the John Radcliffe Hospital in Oxford. It took me almost two hours to get dressed, to have my breakfast brought to me, then rest in order to feel strong enough to attempt any journey out in the car. I had to slide down the stairs (standing was too painful) and then, once in the car, put my feet on the back seat. My mum would drop me off at the main entrance of the hospital and then, gritting my teeth, I walked the 50 or so meters to see Dr A. He had seen me twice in hospital but now, for the first time as an outpatient, I realised that I had made a great achievement. I had managed to sit in a chair for fifty minutes whilst talking to him. That may sound rather odd but it had been almost four months since I had been able to sit in a chair for more than ten or fifteen minutes without being in pain.

The most important aspect of my visits to Dr A was from his idea to make graphs and charts of my accomplishments over the next few weeks. After a four-day assessment of the main activities I could do, particularly how far I could walk and how many minutes I could sit up in a chair, I set myself a target that I had to reach every day. Although progress was obviously slow, at least I could see that I was improving. I also monitored how many times I could go up and down the stairs in a day. As the reader will understand by now, this was a strenuous activity for me. During the six weeks that I saw Dr A, I kept an eye on my weight that slowly increased to a level that I was happier with. I knew that in time I would return to my normal weight. My fifty-minute sessions were very valuable to me, the psychotherapy approach very beneficial. He had the time to listen to, and understand the problems I had, to work through the bad days and try to sort out what led to them. It felt good to talk to someone who was an 'outsider' to my family and friends. Talking to him released some of the frustration and anger that I felt with my illness. Although I found it very difficult to become angry during the session, I always felt a kind of relief when I returned home; my frustration had been shared with someone else.

Dr A took a general history at our first meeting, but because of his profession and the frequency of our meetings his knowledge of my character and personality grew very quickly and at times in very great detail. I realised that no one else in the world knew me as well as he did by the end of the six weeks. I had built up a great deal of trust in him and was upset when he left to pursue his career elsewhere. At the time it seemed as though I had lost a good friend. However, he had decided that I didn't need any further professional help.

My sleeping patterns had never been very good, finding it difficult to fall asleep to begin with as my mind was continually distracted by any thoughts that were troubling me; it was difficult to 'switch off'. Then waking several times during the night, often wide awake, it was not easy to fall back to sleep. These disruptive patterns meant that I rarely awoke feeling refreshed. This obviously affected my behaviour at the start of the day, even more so throughout the period I had been ill. For M.E sufferers, it is vital to get enough sleep. It is a curative process where the body attempts to increase the rate of repair of damaged tissues. For some patients, double their normal sleeping times is still not enough. The complete rest that one gains from a good night's sleep is to recover from past events, essential to those of us who suffered such severe exhaustion mentally and physically after very menial tasks. With a healthy individual, it is often said that too much sleep is a bad thing. However, M.E patients are not healthy and from my experience and reading of other patients' problems, the more sleep, the better.

With Dr A's advice, I had learnt to become involved with my illness, to try to find my own solutions to aid my recovery rather than to keep running back to the doctors who really could not do too much to help. I had to accept my change of lifestyle, living well within the limits of my abilities, learning new routines of rest, exercise and relaxation, and finding new ways of releasing emotional stress, depression and anxiety, all a major factor of my illness.

This was a difficult time for me; it took a lot of courage to accept my condition particularly as I had led such an active lifestyle before I was struck down by M.E. I had no option; if I wanted to get better I had to accept these terms and just wait for nature to take its own course. My GP had mentioned Myalgic Encephalomyelitis to me in April; he said he would give me an address to write to where I could get in contact with other M.E sufferers. I really knew very little about it; it occurred after viral infections such as glandular fever, where the feeling of weakness and fatigue could continue for several weeks or months, but those patients always got better. My GP had never given me a time limit for when he expected to see me recover. Not only would that have been impossible, but it would have been very distressing for me if I had reached the allotted time limit and found myself still very unwell.

Apart from all the physical symptoms of M.E, one of the most distressing facts is that one has no idea how long the illness will last. Unlike a broken leg or recovery from an operation, where there is usually a good prediction of how many weeks will be needed to recover but with M.E it is not like that; the weeks and months and even years slowly dragged on. It was all too easy to give up hope of ever being well again. A patient must hang on to the glimmer of hope and gain as much encouragement as they can from their family and particularly their doctors.

After a further visit to my consultant virologist, he asked if I would be prepared to have a nuclear magnetic resonance scan which can detect metabolic disturbances within the muscle cells. He was very interested to see if the scan would show anything as I was still having so many problems with my legs. I agreed to have the scan but did not receive the appointment for a further five months.

CHAPTER THREE

The uncertainty of British summer sunshine had arrived. I could now walk up the garden (240 steps there and back) and sit in the corner next to the field. I watched the ears of corn blowing in the summer breeze, the red poppy heads and the rustle of harvest mice made a picturesque scene. My thoughts had now turned to the future instead of the earlier pain and despair that I had suffered. I could begin a new day with more optimism and even excitement at the thought of achieving a new goal on my charts.

Setting myself an increment of an extra 40 steps per day, up for fifteen minutes more, and going up and down stairs once more in every four days, I kept up with the targets I had set myself. Consistently walking round with a pen and paper was a tedious routine, but the only way of convincing myself that my condition was improving. Another very important fact was that I never exceeded my daily goal; sitting up an extra twenty to thirty minutes throughout my seventeen-hour day could result in a two-to-three-day relapse. The same applied to my walking; slight over-exertion could result in a several days relapse. The tiredness did not always result immediately after exercise; it could take a week after one strenuous day's activity for it to have an effect on my body. This seems to be one reason why one day I could walk up the garden three times and feel no side effects, but if

I tackled the same exercise three or four days later, I might not be able to complete the three distances, or if I could, might suffer a relapse which might be a setback of two or three days, or even two or three weeks.

There was always the uncertainty of how much the body could tolerate at once, varying from day to day, but in general I learnt how much it could cope with and which types of activity could be carried out with the minimum risk of relapse.

There were several times when I had been so fed up with my condition that I deliberately overdid an activity, mainly because of the severe frustration of feeling well in myself and knowing my legs could normally cope, but this would almost always result in a relapse of one to three weeks depending on the exertion. It was the price I paid and learnt to live with.

Having read many articles and books (in 1987) on 'Post Viral Fatigue Syndrome' (PVFS), there seemed to be two reasons why the excessive tiredness occured; muscle exhaustion after slight activity and a delayed recovery after use. Many patients, including myself, had seen themselves as being unfit (most PVFS sufferers seemed to be very athletic) and so, in order to overcome their difficulty, they at first attempt more exercise as that is what they have been used to doing in the past. The result was often devastating and could cause severe relapses. With the muscles now functioning abnormally, excessive exercise needed to be avoided.

By the beginning of July, I could sit up for three hours a day, walk 700 steps and go up and downstairs three times. Spending more time outside, I began with one trip up the garden and increased week by week. It had been three months since I had driven a car. Feeling very confident, I took my first exercise of the day, walking downstairs and then slowly walking to the car. I smiled as I turned the ignition: it was my first attempt at regaining my independence. I got the feel of the pedals and slowly edged forward onto the quiet road. I only drove a quarter of a mile and then turned back. Using different leg muscles to push down the pedals, unused to this movement for many weeks, I was afraid to exceed my limit. Parking the car, I laughed, partly due to the feeling of freedom I felt but also because the event I had undertaken had been so small in relation to my normal lifestyle. This 'reasoning' was a turning point in the way I felt and thought about my illness. Previously I had been very upset at how little I could do, it was now a challenge and something that I could at times laugh about. From that day on, driving became a new activity on my graphs.

After three weeks, I could drive to the local surgery and back (half a mile) and sit for various lengths of times ranging from ten to fifty minutes in the waiting room, then rest when I returned home. My driving distances increased every two or three days, soon enabling me to drive to the village shops and, as long as I could park fairly close to the entrance, I could do the shopping. To be able to drive again made an enormous difference to me, gaining so much more independence, reminding me of the immense exhilaration and freedom of skiing down a mountain slope as a teenager.

My expeditions to the outpatient clinics at the John Radcliffe Hospital at Oxford were becoming easier to cope with; walking from the entrance (70 steps), being weighed, walking to the virology department (20 steps), and waiting for an average of about one and a half hours. I still had to put my feet up on the back seat of the car for the 20 mile round trip to the hospital, but life was becoming easier and happier.

I lay in the sunshine, contemplating the future, longing for a holiday away from the home that had become almost a prison for me for the last seven months. I'd had to cancel a holiday in Greece, planned for May. Desperately needing a change of scenery, I was determined to go, but was advised against it by my family and agreed it would have been a mistake to attempt the journey. My enthusiasm for travel had temporarily 'blotted out' the reality of my illness. As it happened, the week I was due to go abroad, I was admitted to hospital.

Recalling my last holiday in February, March and April 1986, my second visit to New Zealand, I smiled at the thought of having such a wonderful time, walking the long, almost deserted sandy beaches, breathing in the warm sea air, the sun beating down gaining a golden suntan. My first attempt at drag-net fishing had amazed me. My sister's father-in-law at one end of the net and me at the other, waist deep in the sea, dragging the net across the seabed. To my astonishment, we caught a five-pound 'kahawai' and a couple of crabs. New Zealand is a beautiful country with breath-taking scenery, inspiring for artists. The sunshine, atmosphere and outdoor life had captured my heart. I longed to return for Christmas 1987 for a holiday I well deserved.

My eyesight and concentration had improved but, still finding it difficult to read more than a couple of pages of script at once without getting headaches, I decided at my GP's suggestion that I should have my eyes checked. Chauffeur-driven as usual by my mum, we parked in St. Giles in Oxford. I apprehensively walked the 500 steps to the optician. With so many people around me, cyclists passing on the busy roads, the bustle of city life seemed strange after eight months away from it. My mum departed to do her own shopping. Meanwhile, I only just made it, walking in the optician's door and collapsing onto a nearby chair, exhausted, my legs very weak.

My brothers and sister had a few problems with their eyesight in their early twenties, but fortunately mine were all right. I was told that the eye muscles had been weakened by the virus, just as my legs had been, and they would return to normal as my condition and concentration improved. I was to return for a further check in six months. After meeting my mum, I panicked, feeling so weak that I was afraid that I would not be able to walk the whole way back to the car. I had visions of falling in the street and not being able to regain my strength. Sitting on some steps, I felt worried while my mum walked to the car and drove along to collect me. After returning home, the rest of the day was spent in bed recovering from my adventure in Oxford.

Throughout August my progress continued. During the first week I walked 2,000 steps, climbed the stairs six times, sat up for seven hours, and drove eight miles daily. It took a great deal of determination to persevere with my graphs. There were many days when I'd had enough of monitoring my activities, particularly counting my steps, but once I passed this phase it just became a necessary routine of everyday life. Standing still had also become easier; thirty to forty minutes was my present limit before feeling that my knees were going to give way or become so painful that I had to sit down. I still had bad days, about one in every two or three. Walking up the garden, staring across the acres of fields, I wished I could walk just a little further to the nearby river which I had not seen for almost a year, not since my eighteen month old niece had been fascinated by the darting movements of river life and the ripples left by thrown pebbles.

My short driving distances frustrated me. While I was delighted at being free from home, once again able to do my own shopping in moderation in a nearby market town, I still wanted to be able to go just a little further. Sometimes returning home in tears, either from exhaustion or sheer frustration, feeling so close to returning to the freedom of my normal lifestyle, but in reality so far away from it. At times, I couldn't come to terms with the fact that I could do so little, even though my condition was so much better than it had been all year. My progress was slow, far too slow.

On warm sunny days, I was quite happy to lie in the garden for many hours, passing the long day. The tiredness had lessened, I could talk to visitors for longer periods of time. Walking up the quiet road to the post box (750 steps there and back) was exhausting and at first left me breathless, but I often met villagers who stopped and chatted, always very concerned about me. It was very comforting to know so many people really cared about me; something which would not always come across in everyday life.

Looking back on the eight months I had been ill, my behaviour patterns had altered dramatically. When first feeling unwell, I had been miserable, not understanding my condition, why it went on for so long, leading to a state of complete despair with some suicidal thoughts. Shutting myself away from my friends, putting myself in solitary confinement. My character and personality had completely reversed. I did not like or understand the person I had become. Then as the months passed, after treatment in hospital, my personality slowly showed signs of returning to the person I knew. This role reversal had frightened me immensely, but I began to learn more about myself and other people's lives; how they too must learn to cope in situations of loneliness and despair. I began to learn and understand things I would never normally have had time for.

Finding this subject very interesting, I read books concerning psychiatry and psychology and became so interested in it that I applied for a place at Oxford Brookes University to study Psychology, assuming I would be well enough to do this. However, the places were limited, I did not receive one. In hindsight this was a good thing. My health would have been far too unstable. I was still far more unwell than I realised.

It has been difficult at times to recall events in July and August, my only diary is a note of numerous appointments with doctors. The two months seem 'hazy', rather like trying to recall a good dream you have had; no matter how good you know it was, you can never remember the details. However, I do remember a visit to the dentist. The last time I'd been able to go was in March. Without a fear of dentists, after so many visits throughout my childhood and teenage years, my dentist said I had enough metal in my mouth to sink a battleship! I sat in the chair exhausted from my walk to the department. Although I have stated that I have no fear of dentists, it was impossible to completely relax with the knowledge that yet another filling was needed. Sitting with head tilted back, lights and various instruments stuck in my mouth, extremely weak and not feeling well, the experience was the last thing I needed, but having put off the appointment for so long, I did not know when I would be fit to return.

I walked wearily out of the door saying 'thank you'. Slowly returning to the car, my legs so weak I could barely stand, I collapsed into the front seat. Later, curling up in bed, I fell asleep. It took four days to recover. This event was the first that I recall when I completely lost my voice for four days. Ten days later, feeling stronger, I called in on friends where I'd worked prior to becoming ill. Feeling very enthusiastic, asked if I could help out for a few minutes to see how I got on. After half an hour of tidying up a few things in the office, I had lost all my energy, weary, faint, and with painful legs, I returned home very disappointed at how little I could do outside my home. The following day, I lost my voice again.

Extremely disheartened at my attempts to work, I continued with my usual activities. It was good to see my colleagues, it helped me emotionally to know they were keeping in touch, following my progress and knowing it would be some time before I could return to full-time employment.

Walking 3,500 steps, climbing the stairs 10 times, sitting up for 10 hours and now driving an average of 12 miles daily, my enthusiasm for conquering my illness was becoming apparent. With September upon us and summer drawing to a close, walking up the garden the third time that day, I leant against a tree and watched the powerful combines churning away at the corn, particles of dust flying all around, the grain piling in the trailers alongside. The chaff remaining in parallel rows on the ground. I had always been interested in agriculture and, with so much time on my hands, enjoyed watching the life cycle of an annual crop while sitting at my bedroom window; the ploughs tilling the soil, the sowing and, every few weeks, fertilizing and spraying, the greenery developing and then on to a golden ripe harvest.

The next five days were the best I'd had for nine months. To put it simply, I felt wonderful, full of life, and more alert than I had been in a long time. I looked forward to the prospect of a second attempt at work. Sitting up for three hours in the mornings, feeling so fit and well, I could not make myself stop and relax as I had previously done without fail every day for nine months. I could not believe it! I had no pain in my knees and walked around feeling like a new person. My symptoms had gradually faded as the weeks passed, but now feeling my 'old self' again, life seemed to be too good to be true. My enormous delight, pleasure and relief led me to exceed my limits, I suffered for it drastically.

Sunday the 6th of September. The singing birds awoke me. As I drew back the curtains, the sun peeped out from behind the hazy clouds. It would be a lovely warm day. After dressing I pottered about the house and then decided to go for a drive. I took the country routes whenever possible as avoiding traffic lights meant it was easier on my leg muscles without having to stop so often. I drove for 12 miles and then returned home. Unable to relax after lunch, I drove the car to the end of our lane (about 300 yards) and started to walk up the fields. The hedges were recently cut, the fields harvested, the countryside neat but bare, the view seemed sparse. I walked along slowly, tediously counting the steps. As I reached approximately halfway across the first field (770 steps) I felt a slight twinge in my leg muscles; continuing, the pain increased, so I decided to turn around. It seemed like cramp but unwilling to stop and rest, knowing I might not be able to get up again, I headed back to the car. My legs felt like lead weights. I had pushed myself too far. A horse rider passed by, I considered asking her to give me a lift back, but she had galloped on before I had time to decide.

Stumbling into the car, I drove home, staggered up the stairs, went straight to bed in severe pain. Resting completely all evening and dosed with painkillers I could hardly move. Awake all night in pain, I instinctively knew it would take months to recover. My five days of over-exerting with less relaxation in between resulted in a major relapse; a setback of ten months.

CHAPTER FOUR

An uncomfortable night. Just after 6 a.m. I shuffled to the edge of my bed, carefully stood and, dragging my feet, walked slowly to the bathroom. Returning, I fell back into bed, the dull ache in my leg muscles increasing. A tear trickled down my cheek; how could I face the prospect of several more weeks housebound? I knew it would be weeks rather than a matter of days. Past experience had shown that the pain would not disappear quickly. Lying in bed all day apart from urgent trips to the bathroom, I could barely stand, hanging onto the door handles and propping myself up against the walls. Taking painkillers every four to six hours, my legs were soon immobile.

The following week my symptoms continued to deteriorate. Spending every day lying down, the pain so intense even when still, I became very tearful again. I had suffered enough. My illness had already devastated nine months of my life: why was it happening to me? It seemed as though I was being punished for something; but what had I done to deserve this misery and pain? I had thought that my life was beginning to return to normal but now everything seemed to be falling apart again. Any attempts to work would have to be put aside for several weeks and feelings of guilt crept in after having spent so many months away, but there was nothing I could do.

After several days' rest, the pain became a little easier to bear. Worried about my situation, an appointment was arranged with my doctor's partner, my own GP was on holiday. I do not know how but somehow I managed to struggle to the local surgery driven there by my mum. Fortunately, the waiting room was almost empty. I sat for ten minutes. The pain began to return as I slowly walked into the consulting room. Dr C was very understanding and sympathetic, although by the end of the consultation I was in tears, sitting in a side room while he telephoned the consultant virologist I had seen before. A quarter of an hour later, Dr C suggested that I should have a course of steroids to try to 'pick me up' a little but first I should see the consultant the following week.

The next six days were spent lying motionless on my bed crying, the severe pain had returned, I could barely walk or stand. I was extremely distressed at finding myself with pain as bad as it had been previously in May. Had I set myself back four months? Dr C came to visit me at home. Patiently propped against my bedroom wall, my tearful state was difficult to hide from a doctor who immediately noticed my quivering lips but we had a long easeful conversation.

My anger and frustration at having the Post Viral Fatigue Syndrome (the term at that time used more frequently than 'M.E') re-appeared and was directed straight at my family, in particular my parents. Always feeling guilty after my emotional explosions into tears, I began to hate being so rebellious and not showing an open receiving place in my heart for the love and support my family were giving me. Often trying to hide my feelings, I knew no one really understood what I had to endure. My family and all the doctors were as sympathetic and understanding as anyone could be, but it was not enough. Most people told me, emphasizing it again and again, that I would recover in time. Time – how much time? I understood that things would get better eventually; I did not have a fatal illness, but that just didn't seem to help, it didn't alleviate the strain and stress I was under. If only the doctors had some idea of how long it could take, that would have helped enormously, but they didn't, and of course, it could vary from patient to patient.

Dr C arranged for me to see another psychiatrist: my response was rather unwilling, but I knew that he and everyone else were doing their best to help me in every way they could. I admitted that I needed some sort of aid to pull me through this debilitating illness, having already tried desperately hard to conquer it on my own. Dr A had helped. Maybe someone else could.

Dr O. arrived at my home the next day. It was very difficult to talk to her. Relating my life history in detail was not something I felt I could share with her easily, at least not so soon after having talked to Dr A. An hour and a half later, she left; I was exhausted, crying with fatigue at having had to recall, yet again, the miserable months I had endured. I did not see her again.

Sleeping most of the afternoon, I prepared myself for the journey to the John Radcliffe Hospital the next day. Rising early, the muscle pain was not too bad, but I'd arranged for my dad to meet me and my mum at the entrance of the hospital where I could be pushed to the Virology Department in a wheelchair. (My mum had a back problem and some wheelchairs are awkward to push.) I travelled to the hospital, my usual routine, feet up on the back seat of the car, admiring the scenery as my mum drove along. Various road works and new buildings had appeared out of nowhere since my last visit to Oxford.

Dropped off at the main entrance of the hospital, I walked 15 steps to the reception area and waited for my wheelchair. Later, having been weighed and checked in, I sat patiently waiting to see the consultant Dr P. Already feeling tired, it would have been impossible for me to walk to his department. I had done it many times before but my legs, particularly my knees, were so weak and painful that a wheelchair was a necessity. Dr P was very sympathetic and understanding as always, he explained everything I needed to know about the steroids that I was to begin taking the next day for a two-week course. I was to see him again in three weeks. My morning's exertion had lasted three hours, my body now felt like a lead weight. Returning home, I went straight to bed.

Deep in my heart I expected something wonderful to happen; that I would regain my lost strength and that some of the pain would be alleviated, although I had been assured by Dr P that he could not promise any remarkable results, if indeed any at all. Steroids had helped some patients in the past but it was impossible to know if they would help me. Realistically, I knew and understood this, but some optimism had returned. At least the doctors were trying something else; whether the steroids worked or not, there was at last a little more hope.

Within twenty-four hours of taking the first tablets, I began to notice a difference. Happily, feeling more alive again, I could not believe it! If the tablets continued to have this effect, I would be better in no time! During the next week, my vibrancy calmed down a bit, the muscle and knee pain became more bearable enabling me to walk around upstairs a little more easily.

The tablets benefited my family as well as myself: seeing me a little more confidant, more cheerful and in less pain was a great relief for them. I had been through a great deal of stress, but so had they. My parents had watched their daughter suffer and looked after her almost every need for nine months.

The course of steroids proved to be a valuable, if temporary, relief for all concerned.

My memory betrays me here, recalling little of the next two weeks. My appetite had greatly improved: I weighed just over 7 stones. When my GP visited, he asked me to walk down the stairs, this I did cautiously, still feeling fragile: he was quite impressed as my movements were more relaxed and less 'robotic'. Towards the end of the fortnight, as I slowly weaned myself off the steroids, my mood reversed, tears returned as the tablets were eventually stopped. Severe knee pain came back and the ability to walk had almost ceased.

Three days later, I went back to see Dr P, once again going through the performance of the car journey to hospital, finding a wheelchair and waiting an hour or more in outpatients. The longer I had to wait, the worse the pain. I now recognised most of the hospital staff and even one or two of the patients! As I sat tearfully in Dr P's room, he advised another course of steroids, this time for six weeks, explaining that after that I should not be given any more for several months because of the possibility of unpleasant side effects. I was also given some antidepressant tablets, a two month course to improve my mood also helping as a sedative. Researchers in the United States America had discovered that it had a side effect of helping patients with glandular fever, but the exact benefits remained uncertain. These tablets would take at least three to four weeks to have any effect, so that by the time I stopped the steroids, they would have begun to work.

Leaving the John Radcliffe Hospital, I felt more optimistic, willing and very eager to try anything that might be of benefit to my poor state of health. The steroids again worked very quickly, I felt much better and in less pain within two days of starting the course. Walking around upstairs more easily, now an average of 1100 steps a day and sitting up for four hours, every third day I would manage to walk downstairs once, with great care, holding tightly onto the banister.

Since my severe relapse, I had temporarily given up my charts; they seemed pointless. All I was doing way lying in bed twenty-three hours a day. With new tablets and energy I began a new graph. Three days later, I decided to tackle a visit to the hairdresser in Oxford. As I was feeling very much stronger, my mum drove me to the shops, I walked 20 steps inside and sat down. Apart from visits to the hospital, it had been two months since I had been able to make social visits of my own accord without too much fear of being in pain. One hour later, emerging from the shop, I found that my mum was longer than I had expected returning with the car. I stood, propped against the shop window. After a few seconds the backs of my legs became very painful, feeling like jelly, I thought I was going to collapse. There were no seats nearby and I did not have enough strength to walk back into the shop. Half-standing, in agony, looking up the street wondering where on earth my mum had got to, with my back heavily pressed against the shop window, I could feel myself slowly sliding to the ground. A passer-by looked at me in a strange way, presumably because of my agonised face. Thankfully my mum appeared just before I hit the pavement. Stumbling into the car, I cried.

My visit to the hairdresser had stretched my energy resources too far. Although I hadn't actually walked any further or sat up any more than I would normally have done in a morning, the change of surroundings and atmosphere in a busy shop with murmurs of conversations in the background had made an enormous difference to my usual routine. Maybe it was too soon to attempt such outings, but the steroids had 'picked me up' so much that I desperately wanted to try something outside my home environment which would usually be a fairly minor activity, an everyday affair.

That afternoon as I lay on my bed, the knee and leg muscle pain became intense, the following week proved to be the worst, from the point of view of pain, that I had experienced all year. Lying still, my knees felt internally swollen, the back of my thighs felt tight and very uncomfortable. When trying to move my ankles to change position, I could almost have screamed with the severe tightness that grasped my legs. The steroids had built up water retention, resulting in a balloon-like feeling, ready to burst open. Trying to raise my ankles a little to ease the pressure, tears rolled down my hot flustered face. Unable to move for several hours at a time, I visualised myself as the 'Michelin' man.

Listening to the radio and trying to read could not distract my attention from the unbearable disorder. Already reducing the number of steroids, I still had a further five weeks to go. Very tearful again, I went over and over in my mind all the suffering my weak body had been through and now with this intense bloated feeling pressing against my tender muscles, how much more could I take? When would it ever end?

Gradually reducing the tablets to one twice a day instead of six, the uncomfortable tightness slowly lessened. Over the next few days various visitors arrived, including my GP on two occasions. After a few minutes' conversation, I began to get mild pain in my chest, and gaining enough breath and energy to speak became excessively difficult; so much so that, with breathing so tiring, I gave up trying to talk, it wasn't worth it. My weak body, including my chest, had enough to cope with drawing in oxygen.

Spending my days confined upstairs, usually in my own room, I passed the long hours listening to the radio and reading magazines, reading books required too much concentration, television was kept for the evening, which, whether entertaining or not, at least managed to keep my mind occupied!

My desire to re-learn French from cassettes and a book of exercises was something constructive to fill the long hours. I had passed French O Level five years before. Starting from scratch, I was surprised how much I remembered but I only had enough concentration for twenty or thirty minutes' studying each day. After about five weeks I became too unwell and gave up. My misery was still very apparent, with me crying at some point almost every day, often for no particular reason. On waking, I knew if it was going to be a bad day and, no matter what anyone said or did, nothing could snap me out of my depressive mood. Still finding my mood swings frightening and sometimes embarrassing, I hoped the antidepressant tablets would soon take effect.

The afternoons and early evenings seemed to be the worst times of the day. Awake at 7 a.m., distracting myself most of the morning and then sleeping after lunch, boredom and frustration crept in about teatime every afternoon. Some evenings I would lie on my bed feeling a little miserable and the more evening progressed, the more tears flowed. My parents would try to comfort me but that rarely helped, if ever, the crying would go on until exhaustion took over. Once or twice a week my extreme despair led me to such severe bouts of weeping that I became almost hysterical. That is not something I admit to lightly, still finding it embarrassing to recall such events. The illness had grasped my body and mind in a destructive way making me behave in such an outrageous fashion. It is unpleasant and troubling to find that a usually lively individual can be devastated in such a manner.

At a further visit to Dr P, he brought up again the possibility of a nuclear magnetic resonance scan. When I agreed to undertake this step, he said he would arrange for me to have it as soon as possible.

At this appointment I heard for the first time about injections of gamma globulin. They are injections of antibodies from donors, most of who have had glandular fever in the past and had recovered at a normal rate. This idea was just something to bear in mind, almost, I suppose, a last resort. Dr P was not very keen for me to begin a course until I had finished the steroids and had the scan.

Feeling more optimistic because there was still something that could help me, I returned home more cheerful but, of course, just as weak. Taking fewer steroids my legs slowly began to show some signs of improvement, soon enabling me to walk downstairs once every day, even if only to sit in the kitchen for five minutes before returning to my secluded world. Over the following two weeks, my small exertions included a few steps outside the house, at first just to the corner (20 steps) and then a little further daily. Walking rather tensely, always worried whether I would have the strength to return up the path to the house again, I didn't want anyone's help, desperately needing to regain some of my lost independence. It is a frightening experience to lose that valuable part of you which longs to accomplish everyday menial tasks especially when such skills have been taken away for such long periods.

Throughout the long afternoons, my head tilted towards the window, dark gloomy clouds whispered by. The weather seemed almost insignificant, unable as I was to experience cold winter winds or the soft patter of evening drizzle. One day rolled into the next with little to look forward to. Would the following day prove to be a little better or had I to experience the same miserable routine? It was impossible to know.

Overall, my charts of activity were improving but I found it difficult to keep up with my targets. Since the relapse, my body had been unable to tolerate the regular increment I had set myself. Sitting and walking as often as I could throughout the day, I rarely met my goal. I was afraid of over exhaustion having already seen what it had done to me. Walking an average of 1700 steps, up for five hours and downstairs once a day, I still felt disappointed and disheartened.

Still longing for a holiday it was impossible to even consider a trip to New Zealand in the near future. I was so weak I could not even attempt a couple of days away from my prison to stay with some friends.

The short journey away from home would exhaust me, let alone getting used to new surroundings and talking to different people. It would have been so good for me psychologically to have a change, but I was not ready for it yet.

It is difficult to explain what it is really like spending so much time away from society. You are locked in your own world, protected against the harmful hazards and risks of everyday life. After falling from a horse or bicycle, society tells you to get back on as quickly as possible. The longer it is left, the harder it becomes. This idea is similar to the way I felt about my illness, although I had no option, I could not get back on my feet quickly, I could not get in the car and go off for a drive when I wanted to. Sometimes I did not even have the strength to have a shower. Every day it became just a little harder to fit the role I wished to play and sometimes I even forgot what it used to be like.

Now the beginning of December, the severe knee pain had gradually lessened. The sharp knife feeling stabbing repeatedly in the back of my knees had changed to a dull ache. The uncomfortable bursting of water retention had completely disappeared as I had now stopped the course of steroids. After finishing the tablets, I again became very tearful with occasional hysterical outbursts of crying, still extremely disheartened at the crawling pace of recovery. My parents had reached complete despair watching their daughter entwined in a vicious circle, getting weaker every day whilst resting so much; if up and about a fraction too long her strength giving out completely, resulting in further prolonged periods of rest. My mum often found it too upsetting to come upstairs and see me. My dad and brothers tried to comfort me but were of little help. In the evenings I would often cry, as I have mentioned before, until exhaustion took over. My misery continuing, I increased the antidepressant tablets to two daily, instead of one as suggested. Because of the obvious discomfort I still suffered, the Nuclear Magnetic Resonance scan had been arranged for the following week. Assured by Dr P that the scan would be of little discomfort, I waited eagerly for seven days to see if it would show any significant results.

CHAPTER FIVE

Rain beat against the window as I decided whether I had the strength to visit my colleagues who were having Christmas dinner in a local pub. It wasn't far so my dad drove me. Gritting my teeth and trying to hold back a tear, the knee pain increased. Avoiding puddles, I made my way into the warm, cosy atmosphere of the pub. It seemed strange. It had been four months since I had been able to go out for a drink. Bursts of laughter, lingering smoke, the strong scent of spirits, smiling faces all around.

Although I only managed to stay amongst my friends for about a quarter of an hour, they were thrilled to see me; 'How well you look', 'You've put on some weight!', 'It's great to see you!'. I did look reasonably well, that's often such a problem. My knees certainly weren't. Slowly edging off the seat, rising, I apologised for my short stay and promised I would do my best to attend another party on Christmas Eve.

Back in bed, I lay in pain, my knees so weak I had barely managed to climb the stairs alone. Closing my eyes, I remembered how good it had felt to be amongst friends again, to feel that I belonged. Unable to experience this for many weeks it filled me with warmth to know I was still part of a small community work force.

Exactly one week before Christmas I made my way

to the Radcliffe Infirmary in Oxford. Feeling a little stronger, I had decided I'd try and do without a wheelchair. Driven by my mum, formerly a nursing sister, as usual, we met my dad, a consultant radiologist, who was very interested in the magnetic scan technique. Assured it was not too far to walk, with great determination, one pace slowly in front of the next, I struggled through the long narrow corridors. After about 50 paces a tightening cramp clamped the back of my thighs. Forced to bend my knees a little, I needed to sit down. Feeling faint with weakness I would have fallen in a heap if it had not been for a workman's stool in the corridor. Resting for a few minutes, I dearly wished that I had found a wheelchair.

A few yards away Dr F appeared; struggling to stand upright, I slumped into a welcome chair in his consulting rooms. Later, I lay down with my arm stretched inside the machine at such an awkward angle that it made my neck very uncomfortable. With a rubber ball in my hand, I squeezed it rhythmically, unable to relax, my neck sore and my arm aching. The doctors were unable to achieve any satisfactory results. My arm was too short! Feeling so weak, I cried as I could not stand any more. It was the first time in months that I had attempted to use so much energy, my muscles could not stand the strain.

The magnet measures acidity levels in the muscles. As I had failed to complete the exercise, the only result the doctors could note was that the cells seemed to be normal. As the morning had been unsatisfactory, it was arranged that I should have a body scan three days later. This event proved to be even more traumatic. Lying with my right leg strapped down in a firm position and my foot pressed upright against a wooden pedal, I was eased into a huge metal scanner leaving my neck and head free, a huge wire mesh was placed a foot or so beyond and around my head.

My knees were already painful from having to keep my foot in an upright position for so long before the test even began. Again, rhythmically I had to push down on some weights with my foot. I could feel my muscles being pulled. It hurt. Tears rolled down my face. Every time I pushed down the pain increased. Receiving encouragement from a nearby doctor and knowing how expensive this test was, I gritted my teeth determined to complete the exercises. The weights were made a little heavier. After six or seven pushes, crying, I could not take any more. Exhausted and weak I was taken out of the machine and unstrapped.

Throughout the whole process, lining up instruments and periods of rest being measured in between exercises, I had tolerated about forty minutes. My muscles felt so tender and sore I left the large, hall-like room as quickly as I could. Throughout my entire illness I had never put my muscles through so much pressure. Always agreeing to undertake the scan, I had no idea what my body would have to go through. Thankfully, from the few results taken, there didn't seem to be anything of great concern to show for the experience. The doctors had warned me the scan might not show any abnormality, so I was not worried but, being so conscientious, I felt guilty that I had not been able to complete the required exercise.

Although in considerable discomfort for the next two days, I was very surprised that my legs were still fairly mobile, so much so that for the following day's visit to see Dr P, although a little apprehensive, I again avoided using the wheelchair.

As soon as the gamma globulin arrived from London I was to begin a ten-week course of injections. When I met the immunologist, she and Dr P reminded me that the injections would be very painful and was I sure I wanted to try the course? Eager to try anything, I thought the pain could not really be so bad. The doctors could not promise any remarkable results and told me not to be too disappointed if that was the case. They gave me more charts to record my daily symptoms throughout the ten weeks and to monitor my hoped-for progress.

Returning home, my three visits to outpatients in six days caught up with me. Drained of energy and with my knees burning hot, I tried to sleep. Able to walk an average of 1800 steps during my three-day excursions, I could now, with difficulty, reach 1000 steps. Very weak, I'd had a poor appetite for several weeks and was very miserable.

Unable to attend a luncheon party with my colleagues I tried to gain enough strength and enthusiasm to enjoy Christmas, but that failed to be so. I lost my voice, my temperature was up, my brother had to carry me downstairs to open presents with the rest of the family. Later I spent Christmas dinner lying on a sun bed in the kitchen. Crying most of the holiday weekend, confined upstairs, I had been unwell for just over one year. When would it end?

Taking strong analgesics regularly to ease the extreme discomfort, my muscles were so tender I could barely touch them, they twitched unconsciously. With little in my stomach for four days I was very weak and nauseated when I tried to get up felt faint. My temperature had risen and the terrible headaches I had not experienced for nearly six months returned.

Looking forward to the New Year, I dearly wished it would bring some new hope and encouragement, a new start.

On 31 December my GP and a nurse made a house call with the gamma globulin. I was to receive a 20ml injection in my backside every day for the first five days and thereafter 10ml once a week for nine weeks. The actual injection was not too bad, considering I had little muscle for it to go into, having lost weight. The feeling of someone hammering repeatedly on a large bruise appeared two to three hours later. I was still so weak I could hardly walk and was unable to disperse the fluid. Rubbing the area helped a little but I soon had to lie down. The severe pain increased hourly. Tearfully I remembered the warning I had been given. Taking painkillers every four to six hours, I lay still.

The whole experience had exhausted me but if it was the only possible remaining solution, I was prepared to suffer the consequences. With the injection just after lunch, by about 10.00 p.m. my steps were a little easier but trying to get a good night's sleep was difficult, no matter in which position I lay it always seemed to pull at the muscles leading to the injection site.

New Year's Day, my birthday! I didn't have much to celebrate. Twenty-two years old, I had always thought my twenty-first year would be a good one, but it had turned out to be the worst in my life. Surely this year could not be as bad, could it? The district nurse arrived, apologising for the task she had in hand, especially on a special day. (My GP had thoughtfully suggested that the injection be delayed until the holiday weekend was over, but I was determined to begin them as soon as possible.) A little more prepared for the second injection, the unpleasant bruising pain appeared again about two hours later. Now with both sides of my anatomy feeling very delicate, the third day was one that I would never forget; the most painful day of my life so far.

The injection was placed near to the already fragile first site. This time I felt the needle entering. Later, after walking as much as possible, I returned to bed. With hot water bottles placed beneath the third and still sore second site, I lay tearful. My entire backside seemed as though it had been beaten badly. With so many strong painkillers I was extremely nauseous. Lying immobile, for every slight movement caused unbearable pain and nausea, my tear stained face was cringing. I was so tired. Closing my eyes, I tried to rest; if only I could turn over and sleep. I felt paralysed. My mum sat with me, but soon had to leave as she could not bear to see me suffering so much. My dad had said that if he were in my position, he would have stopped any further injections. I was determined nothing would make me interfere with any treatment. There was no way I could stand many more weeks so dependent on other people for everyday needs. If the gamma globulin helped, all the suffering would have been worthwhile and invaluable.

By midnight the hammering, bruising pain had eased a little. With very slow, gentle movements and all my weight on my hands, I lifted the delicate areas and reversed my position. On my front, tears trickled into the pillow and closing my tired bleary eyes, I tried to sleep. Sleep did not come easily; intense pain always awoke my fragile body.

With my knees burning hot, leg muscles sore, the fourth and fifth 20ml injections were divided into two and this time placed in my thighs. With a pale face and dark circles beneath my eyes, I was thankful the worst injections had now ceased. I could not have stood any more.

With a week to recover before the next 10ml injections were due to begin, my symptoms did seem to be improving; walking an extra 40–50 steps a day, going downstairs twice a day, occasionally three times, even though only for five to ten minutes at a time, and now sitting for five and a half hours; twice that of the previous week. After the sixth injection I could walk at a sedate pace to the end of the garden, needing to rest for a couple of minutes, but this was something I had been unable to achieve for four and a half months. Things really did seem to be improving at last, maybe the New Year had been a good sign after all.

The first three days after the injection were always the best. After that, symptoms returned, by the time the next 10ml injection was due I felt I really needed it. With 5ml in each side and a week to recover in between, I could now tolerate the weekly jab far more easily. Between the sixth and seventh my appetite had improved, my misery became almost extinct, and although my temperature was still up, the persistent headaches and nausea ceased. Now physically able to walk an average of 2100 steps, go downstairs three times a day and sit for six hours, my achievements were greater than they had been throughout my entire relapse. It was still difficult to keep a steady increment, but I really felt my body had at last decided to conquer and overcome this prolonged debilitating illness.

Still unable to drive, for my eighth injection, as I was feeling more confident and stronger, my mum took me to the local surgery; the first outing for five weeks. I was attended to almost immediately, the nurse said I looked much better. I welcomed the return home after only fifteen minutes away. Lying on my bed the back of my knees became warm and uncomfortable. With a hot water bottle on the injection site, my body so heavy with fatigue, I could almost feel myself sinking into the mattress.

Since Christmas, at some point every day, I had lost my voice, it seemed to result from tiredness and was always worse in the latter part of the day. Unable to hold a decent length conversation with anyone, especially when talking on the telephone, it increased the great frustration I was already experiencing. Writing notes to my family to save my voice, it seemed to have disappeared into solitary confinement. After my visit to the surgery, all my strength had left me, needing to cancel an appointment with my GP, I was again unhappy.

This time there seemed to be very little benefit from

the injections. Weaker, unable to sleep very well and with my knees painful I could only go downstairs once a day for a very short period. With the cold unwelcoming winter winds outside, I sat in the kitchen longing for a faster recovery. Due to see Dr P as an outpatient, I was afraid of the consequences. The short journey and visit to the local surgery had set me back. I did not feel my legs could cope, even using a wheelchair, with an excursion to the hospital. I could not stand a further relapse, so I postponed the appointment for three weeks.

After the ninth injection, feeling a little better for the first three days, my charts began to improve. My temperature was down a little for the first time in five weeks, but my loss of voice was frustrating. Over the next two weeks I felt no benefit at all from the gamma globulin. Although I was now able to walk 1850 steps, go downstairs twice, occasionally three times, sit for a total of five to six hours, sometimes walking up the garden twice a day, the severe knee and leg muscle pain was returning. There were soon long periods of the day when I could barely walk or even stand. Only when dosed with painkillers could I attempt to reach my targets. Uncontrollable muscle twitching became more apparent. Crying, everything seemed to be going downhill again.

Extremely worried and anxious about returning to outpatients I spent the third weekend in February in a desperate state. With hysterical outbursts of tears, the knee pain soon grew so intense that I lay, as if paralysed, to try and ease the pain and excessive heat. My legs seemed as though they were on fire. Unable to let anyone touch them, they were desperately tender. What could I do? The injections had been the last resort and now they seemed to have given up on me. Under no circumstances would I attempt the journey to the hospital, I would have spent the entire time screaming with unbearable pain and despair.

My parents were desperate, they could not bear to see their daughter suffering so much. My father discussed the situation with my GP and Dr P, with the outcome that I would be admitted for a third time to the Churchill Hospital for further tests. The journey there was horrendous; sliding downstairs in extreme discomfort, I collapsed at the bottom and had to be hoisted into the car by a helpful neighbour. My idea of staying a couple of days for further blood tests proved to be out of the question. Once in my hospital room I did not leave it for six weeks.

Katie MacLarnon

CHAPTER SIX

The room was in the same corridor as my previous visit. Recognizing most of the staff was a comfort, they remembered me.

Lying in a hot sweat, my knees uncomfortably warm, my thigh and calf muscles so tender with pain drilling through them, a nurse gave me some mild painkillers as I waited for the senior house officer.

Staring at the lime green ceiling and walls, a view I had hoped I would never see again, my eyes filled with water. Doctors and pedestrians crossed the road outside my window. How I longed for the day I could walk again with ease and no pain. An hour or so later Dr O'T took my history, an ordeal I have repeated many times throughout my illness to numerous doctors, yet it was still difficult to recall some of my symptoms and the dates and times they had occurred. My symptoms and achievements varied so much from day to day. His necessary physical routine check-up only amplified the leg muscle pain.

Slowly and apprehensively easing off the bed, I stood so that the doctor could see my delicate condition. After walking two paces with great difficulty, I stumbled back into bed, exhausted, the pain intense. Later, once I was alone, the television on, nothing could distract from the discomfort I felt. Unable to move, my legs were heavy, relaxing was impossible, sleep very difficult.

The next day the consultant virologist Dr P, who knew me quite well by now, arrived on his ward round with four other doctors. He outlined the plan of attack. I thought I'd just be having a few blood tests so was quite taken aback by the suggestion that I should be confined to bed for one week and then try and be a little more mobile the second week, then things would be taken from there. Asking if I agreed to that, I replied that I would do anything that might help improve my condition. In a light-hearted response Dr P and Dr B suggested that I be dangled from the ceiling or have my arms and legs stretched on a wooden board! Laughing, I declined their suggestion.

The following day I received my eleventh injection in eight weeks. As with the previous two it failed to make any noticeable difference to my symptoms, so it was decided that I could stop the almost completed course as it only left me feeling very tender and fatigued. The charts I had kept for the immunologist were generally so erratic that it was difficult to see any conclusive evidence as to whether the gamma globulin had helped my physical symptoms or not.

My appetite was again very poor. I was getting very little sleep, often because of the pain, but also because I was doing nothing to physically tire my body. Unable to do so and with the virus causing fatigue and weakness, I was still locked in a vicious circle. At first I was unhappy at the prospect of staying two weeks, suffering so much, my mental abilities in a rather muddled and confused state. I failed to see the benefit.

With my temperature up again, at least my voice was a little better, although after talking to doctors in the morning, even for just a few minutes, I needed to rest it and could often say very little, if anything, by the time my parents came to visit later in the day.

Approaching the weekend, my knees seemed to be getting worse, taking strong painkillers regularly, the heat was increasing. Every slight movement made the symptoms worse; I couldn't move my toes. Motionless, I lay as if paralysed from the waist down. Tears trickled through my long hair and seeped into the pillows.

By Sunday evening, the pain was so intense I felt desperate. My discomfort was so extreme that a nurse placed a cradle in my bed to raise the sheets. The feeling was as if a knife was ripping down the back of my legs repeatedly, the pain making the tears flow. With so many strong painkillers and a lack of appetite I was extremely nauseous and fatigued from worry and crying. I couldn't recall things ever being so bad. I had never known such pain, the tablets were not helping at all. There was no end to it.

The paralysis frightening me, Dr O'T came to my bedside. Extremely concerned about me and comforting me he prescribed some strong anti-inflammatory tablets. With no visible signs of inflammation my knees felt as though they were on fire. Unable to do any more for me Dr O'T left. After a couple of hours, the tablets had eased the pressure a little, but I had a restless and uncomfortable night.

Awoken at just after 6.00 a.m. my arranged week of bed confinement was behind me, the nurses expected me to be able to walk about 20 steps down the corridor to the shower. I couldn't. Struggling out of bed, leaning on the radiator, then sitting on a nearby chair, I had barely hobbled to the basin to do my teeth. After some consultation I was taken in a wheelchair and sat on a wooden stool under the shower.

Sitting was almost as bad as standing or walking. The feeling as if a sharp knife was being run down the back of my thighs. After my five-minute wash the awaiting bed was very welcoming. At least I could put my feet up again.

After discussion with my doctors, it was arranged that the following day I should have x-rays, an electromyography and a muscle biopsy. I was glad, wanting to make absolutely certain that there was nothing else wrong with me.

The x-rays were taken later that morning. With a blanket around me, tucked into a wheelchair, my journey across to the main hospital was made through the bitter March winds. It made a pleasant change to be out of my room, seeing different people, but the short outing and sitting for about twenty minutes had been very uncomfortable. Back in my room, I was thankful to rest again. Fortunately, the x-rays were normal. Suspicion of the bones thinning due to previous steroids failed to be evident.

That afternoon my mum arrived with some post including some very interesting information on the M.E Action Campaign. Prior to this the only source of articles about M.E that I had seen had appeared in magazines with only a short paragraph acknowledging that the illness was becoming very much apparent, although thorough scientific evidence on the subject was severely lacking.

The Action Campaign gave an excellent summary of all the possible symptoms that patients may suffer, an outline of the possible causes of M.E, advice on how to approach one's sceptical doctor, and the aims of the Campaign.

This information was the first positive article I had come across that greatly enlarged my awareness about M.E, learning of other patients' debilitating symptoms that I thankfully did not suffer from, and also identifying my own individual difficulties with the other thousands of sufferers.

For the first time throughout my illness, I felt I belonged to a unique community, a large group of people that were as unwell as I was. It filled me with enormous strength and encouragement.

As I was still in so much discomfort and barely able to move my legs, a physiotherapist was sent to see me. Her gentle compression when touching my feet and knees was a very unpleasant experience. I couldn't bear anyone or anything touching my delicate frame. Unable to lift my legs more than half an inch off the bed, any gentle exercises were out of the question. Deciding to tackle the situation in a different manner she placed two rubber pads either side of my knee, in turn attached to a small voltage box. The idea was to receive low-level electrical pulses between the two pads that would hopefully distribute the pain. Allowed to alter the frequency myself, even the lowest current was too much for me to bear. I felt as though my tender muscles were being beaten again and again against a wall. As I was unable to tolerate this and since I felt distressed, the physiotherapist left, unable to help me.

As the electromyography study was not due until Monday, I was allowed to go home for the weekend. After the tests, because my condition was deteriorating, I was to be given a week of Acyclovir again, this time a higher does than the previous year, and also a course of steroids.

With the prospect of staying at least one more week I attempted to dress, deciding it would be a pleasant break to return home for a couple of days. After dressing, my body so weak and unused to much movement, I collapsed into bed. Warmth returned to my knees and muscles, it wasn't worth it; the ride in the car would be uncomfortable and how would I get upstairs? Unable to climb them myself, with my legs so tender, the prospect of being carried up alarmed me.

Disappointed and frustrated the intense muscle pain swamped my legs. Movement aggravating my condition, Dr O'T arrived and sat carefully on my bed, his sympathetic nature very comforting, and told me he thought I had made a wise decision to stay in hospital for the weekend.

My room was cheerful and bright with blooming daffodils and get-well cards. Carnations filled the large vase on the windowsill. Watching the buds burst into bloom, the petals fell all too soon.

On Monday morning two paramedics arrived with a stretcher to take me to the Radcliffe Infirmary for the EMG to test my nerve responses. I had never been in an ambulance before and was surprised at the weight of the vehicle on the road, unable to imagine its speed increasing dramatically for an emergency. Driving through the centre of Oxford on a busy morning, the sudden array of crowds seemed strange, almost like being in a different world.

Everyone hurrying past, there were many new shops and arcades, I longed to be up and about again, to browse the enticing windows and walk among the pedestrian bustle.

Pushed along the narrow corridors, I was soon lying with various wires attached to my right leg. Assured that the doctors were passing very low frequencies through it, the sudden shock of the pulse sent pain shooting down to my toes. My knee raised on a cushion, already in extreme discomfort, was then bombarded with sharp pulses that sent my calf and foot flying, my knee already so fragile, I avoided touching it myself. These pulses placed directly on the tender sites were so upsetting to my body that I couldn't stop the tears falling.

In intense pain, it was the worst experience I had been put through. Soon feeling distressed, with more tests on my feet, I was immensely relieved when it was all over. The results, as with all previous tests, again showed no abnormality, in fact, the doctor said I had excellent reflexes.

Back at the Churchill Hospital, my three-hour excursion had drained what little energy I had. Nauseated with fatigue I awaited the final test the following day, the muscle biopsy.

The doctors explained that the test would involve a very fine needle that would leave no scar, so I was horrified when the surgeon pulled out an instrument resembling a pair of pliers. Feeling four or five unpleasant tugs on my tender thigh muscles, the doctor later explained she had been experimenting on a new technique that involved removing larger pieces of muscle.

Recovering from my ordeal, a few hours later a drip of Acyclovir was set up, this time a five-day course, but a higher does than before. I was to also start a course of steroids whilst on the drip, the tablets should help activate the dormant virus and the Acyclovir would hopefully kill it off.

Remembering how much I had benefited from the drip the previous year, I waited eagerly for some sort of transformation in my body. Now used to my surroundings, I was still unable to receive many visitors. With nurses and doctors popping in and out throughout the day I was always fatigued. My dad dropped in for a few minutes at lunchtime and my mum in the afternoons, usually for half an hour, but occasionally just for five minutes.

Unable to sleep much as the evening drip always finished just after midnight and the next one began at 6.00 a.m, it was an exhausting week. Towards the end my face was swollen with side effects from the tablets, I was very tired, and with so many painkillers, extremely nauseous.

As I had been virtually immobile for three weeks, the doctors were concerned about a blood clot, but despite trying to move as much as I could, my symptoms remained unchanged. I had now finished the treatment, unfortunately feeling some side effects. Walking a few steps round my room, the pain was still intense and, feeling so weak, I collapsed onto the bed during the doctors' visit.

Withdrawing from steroids in the past had always resulted in misery even when weaned off them slowly. Now, stopping them all at once, nothing could stop the tears flowing. The four doctors left the room.

The medical SHO returned that afternoon and, sitting at my bedside, spent a long time comforting me and discussing future possibilities that could aid recovery. I agreed to see another psychiatrist. Apprehensive at the idea, I felt I was getting nowhere. Dr O'T was very understanding but he didn't have the time to talk to me at length, which is what I thought I needed, but he did suggest that I should resume keeping daily charts of all my physical activities. I assessed these after three days and then set new targets to be achieved.

I was surprised at how much I could accomplish when seen written down as daily totals; my first assessment day consisted of 80 steps walking round my room, based on walking to the sink, opening windows and turning on the television. To my astonishment, I sat for fifty minutes, even though it was for only two or three minutes at a time. The psychiatrist, Dr M, spent one and a half hours talking to me while I yet again repeated my history, a chore that was beginning to prove irritating for me. This time it seemed more difficult repeating my symptoms and treatments; I then had to describe once again how I felt about my illness, in detail, and what I thought was happening to my muscles when they performed abnormally. My mind was muddled with so many questions, valuable as they were to Dr M's understanding of his new patient. Fatigued, it was a difficult exercise. He decided to return the following week.

My misery had lessened a lot and one week after the Acyclovir I began to notice a difference. The burning muscle pain had improved and walking in my room became a little easier. My body seemed cleansed again and in general I did not feel so unwell. When the doctors came round, for the first time in four weeks, I smiled. They, and the nurses, noticed a great improvement. I seemed to have broken through the barrier of despair.

Reading more material about M.E and watching an excellent interview that a fellow sufferer had given on television, seeing that the general public and doctors were becoming more aware and in most cases accepting that M.E was an illness, my outlook had changed dramatically.

With a far more positive attitude, articles in newspapers and magazines about M.E seemed to appear everywhere. This new publicity helped and thrilled me. For fourteen months I had felt disbelieved, or not understood, by many, although my own GP had confirmed his suspicions many months previously. Now Drs P and O'T had stated that I was suffering from M.E; life at last seemed brighter and more optimistic. The most important and invaluable news was yet to come.

At the end of the fifth week in hospital, I had the news that my blood test was positive, Epstein-Barr Nuclear antibody positive. After fourteen months with no antibodies to fight the virus, my body had now responded. It was the best news. This result was taken from blood at the end of the gamma globulin course; had it helped? No one could ever be certain. Maybe nature had decided to change course and try to fight my debilitating illness at the same time. I believe the injections did help.

Passing the long hours, writing letters was sometimes difficult; my mind seemed muddled and the spelling of each word before writing it needed a lot of thought. This was something I had never experienced before and was worrying at first but soon I remembered that it is not uncommon to experience new symptoms throughout the illness. It did not necessarily mean deterioration. Fortunately, this new symptom only lasted a couple of weeks; although my memory, particularly short term, was poor at times and this was frustrating.

Throughout one of Dr O'T's discussions, he had asked if I had thought about complementary therapy as I'd had all the orthodox treatments currently available with only a little or temporary benefit. This subject was not something that I had thought much about although a good friend of mine, Sally was just then taking a course in complementary therapy, and had a young niece who had been dramatically helped with an ear problem by a reflexologist called Susan K who lived nearby. She came to see me in hospital with the agreement of my consultant, Dr P.

Susan K. gave me a detailed, fascinating insight into her methods of working on feet using her hands; the art of Reflexology. According to the theory behind this, the foot and the hand are maps of reflexes, each part corresponding to all the internal glands and organs in the body. By working on these with various pressures and manipulations of the reflexologist's hands and fingers, nerve function and blood supply improves, helping to achieve relaxation and normal function of all the organs and glands in the body and helping nature to achieve homeostasis. It could also be effective in the relief of pain, but with little clinical research in this field many doctors are sceptical.

I found the experience fascinating and very enjoyable. With caterpillar-like movements all over my foot and ankle, the slight pain I felt was pleasurable even though my feet were still so tender that they could not be moved much. Susan K's movements were very gentle with very little pressure for the first treatment. She spent about forty minutes on each foot, I soon felt extremely relaxed. It was remarkable; waves of calmness flowed through me, the pain had lessened and at the end of the treatment for five minutes I experienced new energy, walking around the hospital room more easily, my slightly sceptical view much diminished. Feeling so much better, I sat up for too long and consequently had a small relapse. Susan explained that normally she would take a detailed history but as I was also seeing a psychiatrist (and I did not want to discuss myself regularly with two advisors), she would put that aside for the time being and concentrate on treatment.

Dr M saw me again and we spoke of my aims to aid my recovery. Talking again about my reaction to my illness and how I felt about it, he wished to see me on a fairly regular basis. I was to continue with my graphs and make some new ones to record particular stages in my walking, which rooms I could walk to, if I could have a shower or not. He wanted to help me, as Dr A had, looking at my bad days and trying to sort out what led to them, why I had relapsed and could they be helped or partially avoided. I arranged to see him in three weeks' time.

Lying patiently, I made a few sketches of my familiar hospital surroundings. My condition was improving, though extremely slowly, I was about to be discharged. The medical staff had done all they could; now it was time to cope on my own again. I would miss the staff community, the gossip, and the happy atmosphere. Even through my extreme suffering, I had welcomed the change from my prison at home and the change to hospital had been of enormous benefit. After six weeks, I felt ready to return; it would not be easy, still unable to do so many things for myself; I dreaded the journey home because I knew it would tire me so much.

The day of my departure was April fool's Day. The previous night, the nursing Sister had placed a dummy body in the room next to mine, the darkened lights just showed the oxygen mask on the face. The result of the night nurse's scream was hilarious; unaware of what was going on, I was wheeled next door to get a terrible fright! But the thought of the night nurse asking the dummy if he would like tea or chocolate was amusing! There was such a commotion that a police officer guarding a special patient came along the corridor to investigate the problem. It was pleasant to end my hospital days with a note of laughter.

Dr O'T came to see me just before I left. His kind words made me more optimistic about the future and it was from him that I gained enough enthusiasm to contemplate writing the story of my illness. I was still unable to walk very far, my brother collected me, still needing a wheelchair, I left the friends I had made and the hospital aroma.

CHAPTER SEVEN

As I was being driven home, I couldn't help but notice the barren winter land that I had left was now luscious green. Coloured arrays in flowerbeds, the smell of fresh cut grass, the sun shone.

Carried up to my room, I welcomed my own bed. Shelves filled with familiar books and ornaments were pleasant to the eye compared with the bare hospital room.

In pain, a little disorientated at first, nausea crept through me. Desperately tired, the short journey from Oxford was nothing in comparison with the distance I felt I had travelled. My mind and body had experienced a thirty-hour flight as though I had gone halfway across the world to see my sister. Feeling jet lagged, I closed my tired eyes.

Over the next four days, the excessive fatigue continued. Determined to make a new start at my recovery I dressed slowly, pulling on 'easy' clothes. I soon slumped back into bed. Days were spent resting and sleeping, always nauseated, I couldn't believe how unsettled my body had again become. Walking to the bathroom was a struggle; my robotic steps returned. Barely able to wash at the basin, the contemplation of a shower was out of the question. My face drawn and pale, dark circles beneath my eyes, it was hard to believe that I was actually a little better than before my visit to hospital.

Back in my secluded world, misery returned, mainly due to the tiredness but already I missed the company of the hospital staff. Their visits only lasted a couple of minutes at a time but were always just right, whereas other visitors often stayed a fraction too long.

Things began to improve after about a week, but one main concern was that my elder sister Sue and her three year old daughter Becky were due to arrive in England at the end of May for a month's holiday. With constant telephone calls throughout my illness, she was always ready to jump on a plane at any time to come and help me, but there was nothing she could do. I wanted to be well enough to enjoy her company and to tolerate a young toddler around the house, Two months was not long for me to improve enough for these simple needs it really concerned me.

Earlier thoughts of writing an article about my illness returned. As I began to make a few rough notes, the idea of a book came to mind. Why not? I had plenty of time to write and plenty to write about! Never having undertaken such a task before, it would be a tremendous challenge. I didn't stop to think about it; I began.

Using a tape recorder, my dad then became my secretary and typed my spoken word. Astonished at how much I could recall, sometimes vaguely, nothing was going to stop me from my new, however temporary career as an author. Me as an author! I would never even have considered it before I had become ill; maybe something good had come out of it after all.

Throughout the second week at home, now able to receive more visitors, I was much happier. When overtired, my voice failed me, but my pace of recovery was acceptable. Sitting up about four hours and walking about 400 steps around the rooms upstairs each day, although going downstairs was still a problem so I avoided it.

Susan K, the reflexologist, made home visits. She also practised homeopathy. Whereas orthodox drugs suppress symptoms, making the patient feel better, homeopaths believe in inducing symptoms similar to those from which the patient suffers, stimulating the immune system to respond to the illness and so overcome it; expelling toxins and disease, symptoms are regarded as a good thing, to be noted in detail. Specifically, which time of the day the symptoms are worse, how they affect the patient, the presence of draughts, and light, different types of headaches, warmth, cold or damp. In this way, a picture of the whole situation is built up and an appropriate remedy prescribed.

Immediately after treatment on my feet, my knees and leg muscles felt warm, I was very relaxed and the pain not uncomfortable. Resting all afternoon, by the evening, the pain had soon gone; more alert and restless, I seemed more myself. It was remarkable! Sitting on my bed, I sang with my records, something I had not felt like doing for weeks.

The recovery was only temporary, over the next three days a cold and slight temperature intervened; although I was walking a bit better, I was generally brighter by the following week. Susan K was delighted with my progress and the symptoms I had had; I was responding well. Feeling better generally, I wanted to begin to withdraw from all my tablets, reducing the antidepressant tablets to one a day and the anti-inflammatory drugs to one daily instead of three.

My recovery changed course during my third week at home. My voice came to an abrupt halt, my chest was very sore while breathing. Seven visitors had drained my energy the previous week in six days, all of whom stayed for about an hour. I knew it had been too much, but it's very difficult to turn visitors away even when you know them very well.

Needing to cancel my visit to Dr M, the psychiatrist at the John Radcliffe Hospital, I postponed my appointment for a week. By then, I had stopped all my antidepressant tablets of my own accord but, because of a chest infection, I had to have antibiotics for a week. The severe weakness and fatigue returned; my physical achievements diminished dramatically. Just when things were going so well, I had been pulled back down. When would I ever be well again?

Susan K continued her weekly visits and helped for a bit each time. After the third session, noticing an inner warmth spreading through me, I relaxed and a few hours later felt much more active. This effect wore off the next day. After four treatments, the good response lasted for two days before symptoms returned again. The benefits gained were a tremendous relief to my system, but discouragement returned as relapse recurred regularly. I needed constant reassurance.

I developed a chest infection. Despite inhalations throughout the day, my chest and larynx were very sore. Still unable to speak, frustration returned. Unable to continue my book for a few days because of fatigue, I then had to begin to write in longhand. Needing to rest my voice as much as possible, I had no idea when I would be able to use a tape recorder again. My chest infection angered me, progress again halted, and a further appointment with Dr M was postponed for some weeks.

As my infection cleared, I was able to walk downstairs once a day to the kitchen, sit for five minutes and then return upstairs, I was out of bed for about four and a half hours a day. But my progress charts were becoming erratic. No matter how hard I tried, on some days I just could not reach my targets, often far below them. I was very discouraged. My fatigue led to extreme nausea. Even lying in bed, when trying to move my legs, I felt as though I would vomit. Severe weaknesses returned. My knees felt 'sick.' In bed for the next three days, I slept most of the morning, awoke for lunch, and then slept for three to four hours. I felt terrible, unable to work on my book, my mind muddled and unable to get rid of the extreme nausea. The antibiotics had not helped the pain in my chest.

My GP made a house call and prescribed a course of anabolic steroids for one month to build up my muscles. My immobility had gone on for a long time; hopefully the tablets would allow me to move about a bit more. My mood had been fairly stable for some time and the new type of steroid tablets were different from those I had been given the year before.

Time was passing rapidly with only two weeks to go before my sister arrived on holiday. I had gained some strength since leaving hospital, but it was still extremely poor. I knew I would have to be particularly careful to spend only short times talking to my sister. It was almost two years since I had last seen her so this would be very difficult. My niece, just three, might prove to be more of a problem.

Within three or four days of starting the new tablets, the pain felt easier and for the first time in many weeks, I was able to walk a short distance up the garden. Although I was outside more, my daily total walking distances were not increasing but I was happier.

Still feeling unable to reach the hospital without causing a major relapse, I telephoned my psychiatrist, explained my condition and my snail's pace recovery, once again postponed my appointment.

At this point, all anti-inflammatory drugs had been stopped; I was only taking the anabolic steroids and a mild relaxant tablet at night to aid my then disrupted sleep. Susan K continued her visits regularly and was delighted with my progress, even though I was unable to see much improvement. She used more and more pressure when working on my feet.

The weather was improving and as the sunshine appeared, I managed to walk downstairs and lie out at the front door enjoying the fresh air. With a pillow to support my knees and a cover on them to prevent the sun bringing too much heat to them, I enjoyed a few days sunbathing. Only able to tolerate about half an hour at a time before feeling too tired with the heat, I began to feel part of my family again; able to lie outside and just listen to their conversation, if too tired to join in before returning to my secluded world.

I wished that the warm weather would continue as I lay waiting excitedly for my sister Sue and my niece to arrive from the airport. Their visit was something I found extremely hard to believe but one I had looked forward to for many months despite my condition.

CHAPTER EIGHT

Overwhelmed and thrilled to see Sue and Becky, tears flowed. Waiting so long to see them, the event seemed unreal. After a few minutes talking, the excitement was already beginning to tire me. The once quite household had come alive again. Becky was so good, but toddlers invariably make a lot of noise at times. Upstairs alone, hearing the murmur of conversation I longed to feel well enough to join in, but I was so tired, I needed to rest.

The following day things went downhill. My two older brothers who live away from home visited, all the family downstairs enjoying themselves, laughing. I lay fatigued, unable to relax, as pain returned. Lunchtime was more dismal. I always had my meal earlier so I could get to sleep by about 12.30 p.m. I needed to and had to rest then. I never went downstairs at that time of day; my daily routine didn't include that, I did not want to disrupt my pattern.

I'd had enough by the next day and cried. Still unused to the noise of chatter, it just wasn't fair! I felt a stranger in my own family. My sister tried to comfort me. Becky stood close by wondering why on earth her aunt cried so much. My family were well aware of my difficulties and isolation, but going downstairs once, sometimes twice a day for ten to fifteen minutes was so tiring I needed to return to bed. I was jealous of my own family. Why should they enjoy themselves so much when I had to suffer? That may sound unfair because they always tried to include me, I know my presence was missed. With my excessive fatigue and nausea, I needed to be alone and quiet.

Sue and Becky came up to see me just a few times a day only for five to ten minutes. They had come so far to see me but I could spend so little time with them.

I read a long and absorbing article that greatly renewed my interest in changing my diet. Realising that the previous week I had eaten an enormous quantity of bread with the result that my symptoms were deteriorating, I seriously began, with my sister's help, to sort out my nutrition. I was determined to try anything. It was difficult at first, knowing what I could and could not eat as so much food contains yeast extract. I began drinking herbal teas. Throughout the first week there were still a few items of food I found difficult to replace until my friend Sally lent me a 'yeast-free' cookery book. Some of the suggested recipes were, to put it mildly, revolting, but others were quite edible. I began, determined to stick to my new diet.

My GP made a further house call and was pleased to see me a little happier. With nothing major to report he would return in a month's time. Susan K, my reflexologist, arrived that morning for a further treatment on my feet. Continuing to feel relaxed throughout and after the session, the pressure she was using was now almost the same as she would use on a patient who was not nearly as unwell as I was. Something inside me must be improving. Her movements used to be ones she would use on a seventy to eighty year old!

Although I was feeling better in myself but still disappointed that my charts were showing little if any improvement, I was reminded that I'd already made a great achievement by stopping all my antidepressant tablets, anti-inflammatory drugs and I had almost finished my course of steroids. I now rarely took strong painkillers, only when the pain was bad enough to make me tearful. Now freed from all those toxins, it would probably take some time for my body to adjust. I must remember all the good points and not just things I could not yet achieve.

That afternoon, after a further reflexology treatment, I was able to walk up to the garage in our garden, approximately halfway from the house to the end of the back garden. I had been unable to achieve this task for four months. I was thrilled. My outlook at last looked a little brighter.

Although my niece Becky vaguely remembered me, not surprisingly, she was a little apprehensive when in my presence, an aunt who was sometimes quite tearful, often in pain, whose voice seemed to disappear frequently, someone who tired very easily and most importantly could not get up and play games with her! She knew I was ill and was in fact very patient with me. Only entering my room with her mother, she was extremely good, but I was very upset. A week of their holiday had gone by, I desperately wanted to be able to see her more and play games with her as my brothers could. Understandably, for the first week, I felt she regarded me as a stranger.

Two days later in an attempt to reconcile my friendship with my niece I entered her bedroom and sat as she bounced on her bed, unwilling to utter any words at first. For the first time alone with her, picking up her toys, I had soon broken the silent and somewhat hesitant barriers. Ten minutes later pain began to creep through my leg muscles. Returning to my room, glancing around, I saw I had left a happy, cheerful little girl who seemed to remember and accept that I wasn't such a bad person after all!

My small adventurous activity resulted in severe knee pain and nausea, but it had all been worthwhile. It was the beginning of a renewed friendship with a delightful young lady who soon adored me and wished to be with me all the time.

Now out of bed approximately four and a half hours daily, sometimes only three hours, I could usually to downstairs twice, but my steps were still erratic and showed little, if any, progress; between 800 and 1150 steps a day. I was a little disappointed but took into account the mental fatigue I suffered whilst playing and listening to my niece. My main achievement was that, once daily, almost without fail, I could reach the garage in our garden to sit for a few minutes before returning.

My chest pain had eased, but still losing my voice when overtired frustrated me. I was beginning to accept the bad days with a little more tolerance. I knew I would have them, it just meant I had done enough activity, however menial, and needed two or three days to catch up again. My recovery the previous year had been too fast. Although I still had bad days, I could always keep up the regular increment on my graphs. Now with my 'up and down' days I believed it was a better and safer way to make progress even though it was almost five times as slow as the previous year.

My few moments with Becky always tired me and soon nausea spread through me. Her little figure appeared at my door more frequently. 'Hello Katie' she would say quietly before entering, awaiting my reply. 'Hello Becky!' I couldn't turn her away all the time, I longed to see her. When would we see each other again? My 'excuse' for some peace was that I needed to sleep. I say 'excuse', it was often true. Her smile faded but picking up her toys, she left with no argument, 'Bye bye Katie!'

One evening, feeling rather low, the last thing I needed was a health programme on TV discussing M.E. I was very pleased at the publicity, but the discussion by a doctor angered me. His attitude was that M.E did not really exist. I thought of all the other thousands of sufferers who might be watching. The attitude of healthy individuals, belief and understanding of M.E, to my mind, had not been helped.

Over the next few days my symptoms began to improve. With the sun shining I was able to lie outside. Feeling better and with a slight suntan, an outsider would never realise I was still so unwell. I managed to sit for half an hour the next day while a local hairdresser came to cut my hair. Later, exhausted, heat returned to my knees. Fatigued, it took three days to recover.

After waking and washing, (the strength for taking a shower was still not possible every morning, even when sitting on a stool underneath it), Becky was soon at my door in time for her pre-breakfast playtime with Mickey Mouse and Joshua the Cabbage Patch doll! She had now learnt that after five to ten minutes she must leave me to rest.

Lying quietly for half an hour I then continued my manuscript. Concentration was always difficult and some events throughout my illness are still very difficult to recall in as much detail as I would like. Extraordinarily, even descriptions of pain that I have endured almost every day for eighteen months, I found it difficult to explain. Now accustomed to it, acceptance was a part of my life, but thankfully the intensity diminishing. Unable to write more than one side of A4 paper a day, my achievements, and accomplishments in tackling such a project were a tremendous enlightenment to me.

Throughout the majority of the fifteen months of my illness, I had been too unwell to have even begun such an exercise. My mind was at last beginning to function again, the confusion and muddled words had almost left me.

Lying in the June sunshine accompanied by my mum and sister, able to relax and enjoy the warmth, we watched Becky pass to and fro on her tricycle. It felt good to be a part of family life once again. My active niece thoroughly enjoyed my company, tiring me immensely at times. She prescribed sweets for me to eat thinking she could make me better! Promising her I would eat them later, I soon returned them to her room, she was unaware of the few extra that she had acquired!.

The summery weather continued, I was much happier until four days before my sister and niece were due to leave on their return trip to New Zealand. The knee pain became intense, my leg muscles ached, headaches returned, and nausea flowed through me. I had done well in accepting a disruptive pattern for a month. The excitement, the increased noise level and further interruptions of my routine for conversations inevitably had all caught up with me.

The day of their departure, needless to say, was a

sad occasion. Becky spent the majority of her last morning with me. How I would miss those huge dark brown enthusiastic, learning eyes, the excited, sometimes lengthy conversations. With her arms full of toys and tears all around they left the English countryside to return to New Zealand, to the country my sister had made her home nine years ago, and to my brother-in-law who had been unable to take enough time off work to visit us.

CHAPTER NINE

New Zealand's awareness and acceptance of M.E at that time seemed to have been more widely publicised than here in the United Kingdom. My sister knew about M.E, one of her neighbours had suffered from it for six months, but of course every case differs enormously, she had learnt even more through staying a month with her unwell sister.

There is so much to learn about an M.E sufferer; I feel it took my parents, who were with me most of the time, over six months to fully understand my complications and difficulties and to really appreciate my rapidly changing behaviour patterns. In the beginning I was sure they had moments of disbelief. I recall them saying many times 'Isn't there anything else wrong?' almost as if to say there must be, 'Our daughter would never behave like this just because she had a prolonged attack of glandular fever.' I think it was particularly hard on them because they are both medical. There must be some medical answer to this, some sort of treatment, but at the time there was 'no scientific evidence' and 'lack of knowledge' were the words of the majority of doctors.

I had arguments with my caring, devoted parents purely from extreme frustration. They were the closest people to me to let off steam. Later, on reflection (then and many years later), I hated myself for putting them through such distress and anxiety, it wasn't fair on them, they were being the best parents anyone could ever ask for or need, I felt I was a horrible daughter. This was one of the hardest parts of my illness to cope with.

My joy and pleasure at the acceptance and recognition by the National Health Service and the Department of Health and Social Security was immense as was the Ten-Minute Rule Bill by Mr J Hood on 23 February 1988, with a second reading that April. The Bill would hopefully lead to greater recognition and further research into the illness and treatment of it.

My own knowledge grows rapidly, my then membership of the M.E Association meant that I received fascinating and excellent articles by sufferers who had got better over time, progress into research, fun and amusing articles as well as the serious, help, advice and, most importantly, support. I learnt about the first reports of this unexplained illness which can be traced back to 1934 in Los Angeles, then Washington, USA in 1953 and a similar outbreak in the Royal Free Hospital in London 1955 where over one hundred nursing staff, struck down by the illness but without a diagnosis of a particular disease, were hailed as neurotic.

Stress seemed to play a major role, the immune system being suppressed at times of peak and prolonged stress. With little medical knowledge available on this subject, I believed there were many other underlying causes. Stress can come under many titles and with many different degrees of it, individuals obviously cope with it in different manners. The illness itself causes extreme stress, the disbelief, uncertainty of the period of illness, coping, lack of support and understanding to mention just a few.

Before I became ill I had been very happy, returning from an incredible solo trip to New Zealand in April 1986. Still unable to decide on a career I wished to pursue, I found myself working in a small nearby town selling china and glass in a characterful building, an old house converted into a shop.

Enjoying the lively surroundings, my health was excellent, apart from an old neck injury, my diet was nutritious. I played squash once or twice a week and, until November of that year, I had felt better than I had done in years, life was exciting and enjoyable.

My appetite for no reason at all soon became poor as we reached the Christmas season at work. Although used to being on my feet all day, I was putting in a few extra hours that I was happy to do. I wasn't sleeping well and was over tired. Tonsillitis and then glandular fever were prolonged into the Post Viral Fatigue Syndrome/M.E.

I have been deeply saddened when reading of the few young men and women who have been driven to suicide. Their severe distress at being so unwell, and disbelief by many led them to end their short lives. An illness that can do so much damage and harm emotionally is devastating. I too found myself at that extreme depth of despair but ironically at that point was too ill to go through with taking my own life. I was too weak to open my bedside table drawer, let alone open a sealed brand new bottle of 28 sleeping tablets. If I had, due to my parents then routine of saying goodnight then leaving me until the next morning, I wouldn't have been found until it was too late.

I am lucky, I have pulled through the worst even though my struggle remains difficult at times and is a very long process. I was very fortunate to have been diagnosed as having glandular fever so early on in my illness, at least I had some evidence that something was wrong, I was ill. Many sufferers experience months and years with no idea, no evidence of an illness, a traumatic event in their lifetime that I believe only someone who has experienced M.E can really understand and appreciate.

Early diagnosis, although sometimes difficult, is vital. I was given the wrong advice in the early stages of my illness. Friends thought that, if my legs were so weak, surely exercise was the answer, it seemed logical. Towards the end of my parents' holiday in New Zealand I remember telephoning my dad to be given advice to use the exercise bicycle we had. It was impossible for him to understand or even contemplate that I couldn't even push one pedal down let alone round and round. This was the first time I learnt that exercise was absolutely out of the question. The virus lay dormant most of the time until any form of bodily movement would make it active again, resulting in either immediate muscle weakness and pain, or a delayed reaction up to a week later.

Watching the rain through the kitchen window beat down, the darting splash of the car wheels pass by. I love driving. The previous summer I was often able to drive away from my surroundings more than I could walk. Maybe I could do that again in the next two or three months? It was a challenge I longed to overcome.

I'd been exhausted since my sister's departure, my energy drained from me and suffering extreme nausea. Watching Wimbledon on television I felt the desire to play tennis again, the exciting rallies, admiration for the best tennis players in the world. When I was fourteen years old I'd always dreamed of playing on the famous sports ground. Concentrating was too hard, with the ball spinning back and forth, migraine clamped down on my forehead. After one week of unsettlement and one of constant sleeping and rest, my quiet daily routines returned to normal.

EPILOGUE ONE

Waking at 7.00 a.m. I washed and dressed and then had to rest for an hour before continuing with my daily activities. Reading magazines, books and writing letters took up most of the morning accompanied by the radio. I sat upright with my legs straight on my bed, or in my brother's room as it is larger and brighter, vacant since he left home. I could only sit for half an hour at a time as any longer brought on pain.

Standing wasn't easy, seven to eight minutes was my limit. It had always been harder to achieve, often more difficult than walking. My meals were always brought to me although I had a small kettle in my room and a box full of rice cakes and bran biscuits allowing me to make my own breakfast.

Resting for one and a half hours after lunch, I'd then try and go downstairs for the first or second time that day. On a good day I'd walk outside as far as I could, sometimes able to reach the end of the garden, a task I'd been unable to achieve for five and a half months. Soon I hoped to begin short trips out in the car, leaving my prison for a short while.

I was beginning to feel a part of society again after missing out on it for so long. I often wondered whether I'd had the chance to mature on my own, but I know my ability to cope with my illness had helped me do that.

Listening to the radio in the afternoons to a

programme that always amused me, I sometimes looked through mail order catalogues. I loved receiving post and it brightened up my day a little.

Deep in thought I watched the clouds glide by, the trees gently swaying, the birds swooping in for a place on the telegraph wires and the tractors trundling in and out of the farm in desperation for the rainy days to clear. During the evenings watching television and listening to favourite records passed my long day.

Out of bed approximately four and three-quarter hours daily, although sometimes very much less, I was able to go downstairs two to three times and walk approximately 1200 steps out of an estimated daily average of 10 - 15,000 when healthy. I continued with my graphs; they had been a valuable part of my recovery process.

My tearful hysteria had changed dramatically to a few soft tears once in a while. I preferred to be quiet and often alone. The muscle and particularly knee pain had lessened although some days were obviously worse than others.

Sleep was still often disrupted but had improved. If I had an unsettled night, my symptoms tended to be worse the next day. My concentration, appetite and strength continued to progress. As long as I took life at my own pace (no one should tell me what I can or cannot do), my outlook appeared much brighter and more optimistic.

In general, with all my symptoms improving, however slowly, I'd learnt to tolerate my bad days. I had to; I still had many. A few grey hairs had appeared amongst my dark brown ones, but I pulled them out and hoped they would stay away for a few more years! I resumed my meetings with Dr M but not until I felt I had the strength to make a return journey to Oxford and was able to talk for fifty minutes without tiring too much. I hoped my need to see a psychiatrist would not last too long.

It had been three and a half months since I'd left hospital, I had rarely felt the need to talk to him. I was at last fighting my once losing battle; instead of one step forwards and three steps backward, it was two steps forwards and one backwards. My change of lifestyle had obviously been very dramatic but I could accept that, although I had to admit jealousy sometimes burst out when friends, or my family, went somewhere I really wanted to and couldn't, well, not just then.

I missed going to parties, meeting people, dancing. At twenty-two I felt I'd experienced the life of a not-so active eighty-two or ninety-two year old. But maybe that is a blessing in disguise. I appreciated life more than I ever used to, every day when I felt just a little better, it was of great value to me. My eyes seemed to search around and take in more. I could stare at a vase of flowers and think how beautiful they were while before I really didn't pay much attention to their beauty. A very dear friend of mine, Annemarie, whom I'd known for seventeen years, brought me a huge bouquet of flowers when I was in hospital. Looking at their delicate but sturdy framework helped to pass the time.

My admiration for those people who will remain unwell for the rest of their lives with terminal illnesses and other individuals who are bound to a wheelchair is great. The way in which our bodies soon adjust and learn to cope really is quite remarkable. I sometimes feel angry and bitter at having this illness, why me? It is clearly something I would have avoided if possible, but I knew I'd learnt many things from it. I took every day as it came, it was very difficult for me to keep to certain arrangements and plans. My future was very unpredictable, my health was and is the most important aspect of my life and for me it must remain so.

In general I looked very well, although I noticeably looked very tired after over-exertion. To express my appreciation for the love and support my family have given me goes without saying, I couldn't have managed alone. I have been very fortunate to have a good secure home to live in and caring friends all around me. My parents and I had some difficult times together because of my illness, sometimes it was like walking around with a brick wall between us. At times we needed space from each other, but I could never get away. I'm sure that is only natural and inevitable after eighteen months constantly together. I think we all coped very well.

My GP was undoubtedly very valuable. His immense and constant support and belief that I was genuinely very unwell from the early stages of my illness always gave me a little bit of strength to pull through. My thanks must also go to the many other doctors I saw who always tried to do their very best for me. Also, to the lady who patiently and efficiently typed the manuscript for my first publication.

Many doctors remained sceptical at that time; this angered me. I wish to stress again as I come to the end of the first part of my story that I was a very happy, healthy, lively, athletic individual before I was struck down by M.E. Always enthusiastic but not one looking for great achievements to be let down if failure occurred. I had been and remained very unwell. I was living proof of that.

My drive to continue my life happily and healthily remained so strong. Medical research and knowledge continue to improve. My aim was to return for a well-deserved holiday to New Zealand in the future. I was determined to make it as soon as possible. Full-time work seemed like a dream, but I'd every hope that one day I'd manage it again. My employer kindly kept my job open for me, with the knowledge I could start with just a few hours a week, when I was well enough, it took some pressure off me. My gratitude to him is obvious; knowing I still had a job had taken a great deal of would-be strain away from my illness.

I received an 'Invalidity Benefit' meaning that I acquired a regular sum of money each week. I was very fortunate to have the financial support of my parents.

I believed it would take the best part of a year to really see a great improvement and then possibly a few years after that for a full recovery, but I was prepared for that. I knew in my heart that things would work out for me eventually, in my own time. ONE DAY I KNEW I WOULD BE WELL AGAIN.

PART TWO

CHAPTER TEN

Part One was published during the summer of 1988. It was difficult to find a publisher but eventually I found a small company willing to accept my book. Unfortunately, just after it was printed the company folded, leaving me to promote and sell 400 books. My parents helped me with this task, distributing to libraries and bookshops from one end of the country to another. The whole process of writing my story and seeing it through to print had been an interesting experience, but it was too much for me and led to a severe relapse taking a year to recover.

My desperation to regain lost strength led to a conversation with my GP inquiring about complementary medicine. He suggested I see a colleague of his from Oxford who used acupuncture. In April 1989 Kim came to visit me. He was a doctor working in neurology but had a great interest in all aspects of medicine. I warmed to his calm and caring nature immediately. My medical history was related yet again, not an easy task as I had so little energy and my voice was barely audible. Kim talked to my parents of his concerns for me, he felt he couldn't just walk away from such an unwell person knowing that no one else had been able to help me. This first meeting was the start of a long rewarding friendship with a doctor who undoubtedly had a vocation in life to help people.

One day in early July Kim phoned, he was unable to visit me and suggested it was time that I tried going to see him for acupuncture and advice on learning breathing techniques. Apprehensive, I thought it over for a couple of hours and decided it was a task I needed to try.

My mum drove me the eight miles to Marston. With the window wide open, the wind blew through my hair twisting it in all directions. It was a welcome relief from the humid, sticky 92 degrees outside. The roads were very busy. It was a holiday weekend. I found it hard to obscure mentally the stream of cars coming in the opposite direction, so I looked out at the surrounding fields. As I got out of the car my legs ached. I walked into Kim's house and flopped onto the sofa. I was shattered and desperately needed to lie down. Kim took me upstairs and began my relaxation session. One hour later my own bed welcomed me. I was pleased at the achievement I'd made but this brief journey had exhausted me.

A couple of days later after rising at 7.00 a.m, having my breakfast and a shower, I fell asleep again and didn't wake until 11.00 a.m. I decided to tackle a new challenge. Walking a little shakily downstairs I got into the car and headed towards the local Post Office. Parking several yards from the shop, I felt almost conspicuous because it was such a strange thing for me to be doing, walking into a shop and doing my own shopping, unaided. Returning home, I sat for a few minutes before lying down to rest. It took 4 hours to recover.

The following morning, after a restless night, I seemed stronger but decided to take it easy. The sun couldn't decide whether to shine or hide behind clouds, but I lay outside when it appeared. By 8.00p.m. The summer evening was drawing in. I strolled up the garden and sat in the chair at the corner by the field. The grass was dry and scorched; pinecones lay here and there. Flies surrounded me, attracted to my white shorts, the sun highlighted the far side of the field. Glancing through the branches of a fir tree, I watched a light aircraft humming past, and could hear cattle being rounded up in a field beyond. Rising, surveying the newly harvested field, our cat Maxwell's black and white head appeared, he was stalking something. A moment later he flew through the air and landed heavily a couple of feet away. I couldn't see if he had caught anything, but he must have been dissatisfied, for a few minutes later he appeared in the kitchen as I made my way upstairs.

Kim came out to give me another treatment in acupuncture, my seventh session. He placed one needle in the centre of my throat, one above my lip, two either side at the base of my nose, one in my forehead, one in my skull and one in each wrist. I was rather startled at first, they were sore points, tears trickled down my cheeks. Kim was thrilled at my physical reaction; my pulse was much stronger and more regular and I could actually feel my heart almost jumping out of me! The needles were taken out after about 20 minutes. I was relieved even though I had been very relaxed during the treatment. Kim was astonished at how well I looked, my complexion was clearer and my eyes sparkled. I looked so well. It was hard to believe. Tired, I felt stronger inside.

CHAPTER ELEVEN

August, the nights were a little cooler, sullen clouds greeted me when I pulled back the curtains in the mornings, the wind had picked up, after only a week of the sun's absence my skin longed to feel its warmth again. My walking distances were continuing to improve reaching an average of 1100 steps a day. I was sitting for approximately four and a half hours and had just begun to go downstairs for a third time each day. My progress delighted me. With great effort and perseverance, I attended my best friend's wedding. I had been looking forward to it for several weeks but was worried whether I was fit enough to manage. Annemarie and I had been very close since we were age five and six years old and as little girls had chatted excitedly about the day we would marry. Her day had arrived, she looked beautiful and radiant, and I was thrilled for her.

Sitting throughout the ceremony my energy was soon depleted. I put on a brave face smiling for the photos and then returned home accompanied by my mum and dad. Annemarie and Greg had been back from their honeymoon a fortnight, I telephoned only to become quite envious of their holiday, windsurfing, sailing, water-skiing, scuba-diving and horse-riding. I imagined the clear blue warm sea, beautiful white sandy beaches, sunshine, palm trees, I hoped that one day I too would visit these exotic climes.

Over the next week I made an effort to drive every other day no matter how short the distance. The Department of Health and Social Security had sent me an allowance book, so instead of sending me a cheque every week for my invalidity benefit I now had to go to the local Post Office every Thursday to collect my money. I incorporated this into my driving achievements. The further I drove the more confident I became but now, instead of worrying about whether my legs were strong enough or not, I started to worry about my concentration. Every now and again I would suddenly become very tired, just for a second, but enough to be worried that for a moment I had lost concentration on my driving skills. My brain was unused to focusing and paying attention to so many things at once. It was scary, so I tried to make sure I always had a passenger with me when going somewhere new or a little further for the first time, until I became less tired.

Kim continued to come out and visit, giving me acupressure for the second time as he had forgotten his acupuncture needles. As usual with all his therapy I soon felt relaxed, it made a pleasant change to get a good night's sleep afterwards.

A couple of days later I received a surprise, flicking through our local newspaper I came across an article about myself. A reporter from the 'Oxford Mail' had telephoned me a few weeks earlier saying that she may do an article on my book, I hadn't really expected anything to come of it but she had given me a good review. I had just sold out of my 400 books, reprints would be very expensive. With more books on M.E being written all the time, demand for mine wasn't so high.

The following day, feeling much stronger, I decided it was time my driving distances should be increased. With my mum as a passenger I drove her five miles to a small nearby town. Sitting in the car whilst she did some shopping I was confident and reasonably cheerful, it wasn't until I'd driven just over seven miles that my legs started to feel uncomfortably tight and aching. Easing up the driveway and turning off the ignition, I sat for a few minutes taking deep breaths. One hour later I was sound asleep, unaware of how tired my body had become from my morning excursion.

By mid-afternoon, finding it difficult to open my sleepy eyes at first, I awoke in time to listen to my favourite radio programme. Lying still for a while collecting my thoughts, I was keen to tackle something else, but had I already done enough for one day? Driving nine miles, it was the furthest I had been for two years. Making a snap decision I telephoned Sally. She was overwhelmed and excited when I said that I wanted her to take me out for a quick drink in one of the village pubs later that evening. She couldn't believe what she was hearing, I too began to wonder if I had made the right decision as I became very nervous and uptight as 7 o'clock approached.

My legs and knees ached, I thought partly just apprehension and rightly so, it was about twenty months since I'd been into a pub. Walking inside I soon relaxed. With a glass of mineral water clasped in my hand, we returned to the summer evening fresh air and sat on a wooden bench by the car park. The minutes seemed to pass quite quickly, after a quarter of an hour my concentration started to fluctuate, smiling became more of an effort, and my thoughts were wandering. After thirty-five minutes we were back in the car on our way home. Slowly walking upstairs to my room, suddenly tired, I lay down for over an hour and watched the television. I was thrilled at my achievement, it was the start to regain a social life, and I'd felt good being out, I felt good about myself. With a good night's sleep behind me, I slackened my pace the next day.

The end of another month. The evenings became cooler, the infuriating insects that lined my ceiling every evening were either staying on the other side of my window or crawled back into the woodwork. I hate grasshoppers and was thankful the necessity to scan my room for them before retiring was over, I couldn't bear them when they jumped on my pillow, or me in the middle of the night! Switching off the television and reaching down to the floor to turn off my bedside light, the night was calm and quiet.

CHAPTER TWELVE

The familiar sound of cock-a-doodle-doo awoke me at 5.30 a.m. made by a cockerel belonging to one of the neighbours. The autumn light glinted through a crack in the top of the curtains; clutching the duvet with my arms I rolled over and fell asleep for another hour.

It was time to continue my progress. Driving at night would be the next hurdle to cross. It was exactly two years since I'd been out into the darkness alone. My knees and legs felt tight with nerves, but I forced myself to get into the car, needing a few moments to recall where the lights were.

Reversing slowly out of the drive, easing down the quiet road it seemed bizarre. Once on the main road everything appeared to be going faster than usual. A sense of further independence struck me, alone with the car and just bright lights around me. Driving into the darkness was fun! Something that startled me most was the fact that I was unhindered by the gleaming lights from street lamps or passing cars, by the time I returned home I was surprised, stunned, to find I seemed far more alert. I had expected to feel very tired, but I felt great. I had driven a round trip of six miles, pushed my legs through a mild pain barrier and was home again feeling fine. Sleep came easily that night and the next two days.

My walking distances had remained stable for some

time, I needed to stride away from the secure surroundings of our house and garden. It wasn't an easy thing to do but at least there was now only a tiny part of me that was afraid of stepping out into the unknown, of being well and fit again.

Some friends down the road were away for the weekend and Bundle their cat needed feeding. The familiar feeling of nerves hit me as I slowly paced along the road. Breathing deeply, after a few steps my head began to swim and my eyes blur. I was within twenty feet of the house and thought any second I would faint but somehow I pushed myself through these symptoms and soon collapsed into a deck chair at the back of their house.

My mum had cycled beside me, she proceeded to feed the beautiful blue-eyed Bundle. I sat with my head between my knees for a couple of minutes. I walked back alone, stronger and more confident, returned to bed, one and a half hours later, tired eyes closed.

My stroll down the road had been the furthest I had walked for exactly two years, my muscles were a little stiff and warm which was only to be expected, but it was yet another new achievement. I was thrilled and it greatly pleased my parents too, to see their once and not so long ago fragile daughter walking along the road again.

CHAPTER THIRTEEN

The car pulled into the drive, my delighted mum welcomed two tired travellers. I waved from the window to my elder sister who hadn't and never seemed to change a bit, apart from the added weight of being five months pregnant! We met at the stairs and exchanged greetings. Becky had naturally grown in height and her hair was longer and darker. My emotions were mixed. I was so happy to see them, excited, but I felt so unwell I wasn't really in the mood to see anyone.

The happy adorable little girl pottered around upstairs for a while, getting used to her new surroundings, walking in and out of my room three or four times for a quick chat. Although I desperately longed to renew my friendship with my niece I couldn't cope any more, not wanting to shut my door and keep her out. She had no idea what sort of condition her aunt was in; she was far too young to understand. Over the next few days, I found the noise difficult to handle. At times Becky rode her tricycle and had fun on the swing her granddad had made at the end of the garden, this gave me brief interludes of quietness.

The autumn red and mustard-coloured leaves looked beautiful in the sunshine. Most of the trees were now sparse; their bony-fingered structures empty for another year. The seedlings in the field were growing fast, green shoots rippled in the breeze whilst pheasants mingled together searching for food amongst the new growth. The contrasting colours of the dark and golden-brown birds, the bright green fields and orangey reds of the trees in the woods beyond was pleasing to the eye.

Winter gales temporarily interrupted the autumn calm. Rain beat heavily on the ground, lashed against the windows, even the strongest trees swayed to and fro. Flowerpots and a plastic watering can were blown out of the open garage, tossed amongst armfuls of leaves. For two days the gales blew and then the warmth returned. Clear blue skies in the afternoons, it was hard to believe it was almost November.

I joined my family outside to be videoed by Ian and Julie. Sue wanted to take a film of us all back to her husband Dave. I had never been 'on camera' before and once I had got over the shock of seeing myself looking so awful on the video, I was taken aback at seeing myself walking! I looked like a 'normal' person walking, bending, and kneeling with no robotic steps as in my earlier years of illness. I was amazed!

I tried to spend as much time as I could with Sue and Becky during their last two days. I had found it very hard at times to tolerate extra company in the house and it's more tiring listening to a child talking and chattering than to an adult, but I know living with them for a month had been good for me. Sue had noticed a great difference in my health and said I looked much better and was happier, smiled and laughed more frequently.

Sue and I talked for a while before she left, our last sisterly chat for another year or so. I could feel tears looming up inside me but held them back. After collecting her bits and pieces together, familiar little footsteps padded up the stairs for the last time, Becky said goodbye as tears filled my eyes hugging her. I walked into the spare room with a couple of tissues scrunched up in my hand, watching and waving as Ian and Julie eased down the drive in Dad's car taking them to the airport.

The clocks had changed the previous weekend, darkness arriving by 5.30 p.m. Long winter nights were upon us once again, street lights shone and glistened in the puddles below.

Katie MacLarnon

CHAPTER FOURTEEN

I hated getting up on cold mornings, wrapping my large spotty cotton dressing gown around me snugly on the way to the bathroom to have a shower. There had been so many times during my illness when I had been barely able to wash due to lack of energy and chronic weakness, but now I could shower daily; it was a wonderful, if only simple, step forward.

Sitting upright on my bed looking out into the dense November fog, my thoughts drifted over the constant nightmare I had suffered for three years. Three years of physical and emotional pain, fear, anger, worry, persistently fighting against a devastating illness that had refused to leave my body and let me lead a normal lifestyle. It was a very long time. I compared it to that of the three years prior to my illness; my final year at school, having fun, always amongst friends, laughing, playing sports, studying, passing A-levels. At nineteen going to secretarial college, passing more examinations, making my first visit to New Zealand, quite a challenge on my own. At that time travelling to the other side of the world was still an unusual adventure, not a common occurrence as it is today. I returned home, looking for work. I took on a temporary job, then nine months later, a second wonderful three month stay in New Zealand. Enjoyable years for a young athletic intelligent woman.

There was no comparison, my years with M.E, although traumatic, were almost a blank, a horrific emptiness, and a void that I now could barely place. It seemed as though three years of my life had gone missing. With my 24th birthday approaching I still felt as though I should be nearing my 21st.

At times I couldn't help thinking those years had been wasted, but at the same time I had learnt more about myself, found far more courage and determination than I had ever realised, and had become far more compassionate. I began to understand how important life is, to be healthy and live life to the full, to really enjoy even the smallest of events, to face difficulties and learn to cope, trying to overcome them if possible.

Kim kept telling me my experiences would be invaluable later on in life. I was sure he was right, but for now it was still so hard at times watching my friends getting on with their lives, getting married and settling down, finding themselves in good careers with good prospects, but my time would come, I just had to be patient.

Christmas was near, it made a wonderful change to be able to see all the decorations in local shops, bright colourful displays. It was easier this year to enjoy the atmosphere, the previous three years I had been too ill to take in the merriment of the season.

On Christmas Eve I'd decided to have a quiet restful day enabling me to have a more cheerful time for

Christmas, but my best friend Annemarie had other plans! She arrived out of the blue with her husband, Greg, and one of her brothers, Mark. It was a wonderful surprise, but I shook with weakness all of the twenty minutes they were here. I hadn't seen my good friends for nearly six months since their wedding, for one reason or another, but we always kept in touch regularly by letter or phone. I was thrilled to see them all. Annemarie had brought me a huge, beautiful bouquet of flowers and for a Christmas present, two lovely photographs taken at their wedding.

On 25 December I wandered downstairs to join Mum, Dad, Alistair, Ian and Julie to open presents. As I opened the colourful wrappings, flashbacks of last year kept appearing in my mind; my body had been so weak, my arms and hands not strong enough to reveal the gifts my family had given me. Tears had flowed rapidly; it had been an unhappy day for me.

I didn't feel able to go downstairs for lunch, needing to rest, and welcomed the quietness of my room. By late afternoon tiredness caught up with me and after a brief visit from one of my aunts I couldn't control the inevitable tears from sheer exhaustion.

The final few days of 1989 were spent resting and sleeping in my peaceful, cosy room. Soft white clouds melted into dark looming ones; my tired hazel eyes followed the last of the rain droplets racing in wiggly lines down the windowpanes. The end of another year another decade, the end of the worst of my illness? I hoped so.

CHAPTER FIFTEEN

1 January 1990, my 24th birthday. A new calendar year and a new birth year. Psychologically a new beginning, not just for myself but also for everyone. I was unsure how I would feel at the start of this new decade but was thrilled to awaken with a fresh and exciting approach to life ahead, particularly in handling my illness. I dearly hoped these emotions would last.

February came and went quickly, my sister Sue had a baby boy, Alex. My dad retired after forty years in the medical profession, formerly as a general practitioner and for the previous fifteen years as consultant radiologist. Meanwhile my recovery made steady and welcome progress. I had devised a new plan of attack, instead of trying to increase my walking steps and driving distances all at once I set aside seven to ten days of making a determined effort to tackle one task at a time. I began to feel very different in myself, much happier and more confident in my recovery.

With spring upon us, the weather was becoming warmer and quite sunny. The strong gales of the past four months had thankfully lessened to a light breeze. Bird songs woke me in the mornings, buds rapidly emerged after the mild winter.

In early May my dad was elected as a district county councilor. I was so proud of him. He was a good listener and prepared to take on board everyone's opinions about different issues and hopefully arrive at an unbiased outcome. He was still working part-time at the Oxford Hospitals, the hours put in as a councilor kept him busy.

My days continued much the same, a few good, a few bad. Summer passed by unremarkably. My walking distances were improving, I could now manage half a mile, still needing to rest as soon as I returned home again. By the following March this goal was reached three times a week. I was thrilled.

My friend Sally was to be married in a church in the next village. She has been a family friend for as long as I can remember. Eight years older than myself she had grown up with my sister and elder brother. Sally had given me a great deal of support during my illness, so I was excited to be able to manage to attend the wedding ceremony with my mum and dad on a bitterly cold April day. Although the reception was only a few yards along the road from our house I didn't have the energy or stamina to attend.

The spring and summer were spent concentrating on driving and walking, trying to increase my distances. I was happy, as much as I could be having so many restrictions still imposed on me through weakness and fatigue. I bought a new camera and took pictures of the local areas I could walk to. Things were good. As autumn approached I drove to Oxford (twelve miles) for the first time in five years, returning without shopping, my energy still too low to drive such a distance and shop. With such excitement at my achievement I wanted to sing along to the car radio but even singing was too much of an effort, all my energy had been used concentrating on driving my car and myself home in one piece. That afternoon disappeared in a deep sleep.

Just before Christmas a dental abscess forced me to the dentist's chair. For four years I'd missed out on check-ups my dental care had suffered because of my illness. In the early years I hadn't had the energy to lift a toothbrush to clean my teeth for days at a time. Five fillings were needed, it took until the following May to complete this process due to the exhaustion suffered after each visit. Kim helped me through it with acupuncture and homeopathic remedies.

In November my beloved cat Maxwell suddenly became ill. His youthful appearance belied his seventeen years. A liver tumour grew rapidly and on Friday 13th my dad had the unenviable task of taking him to the vets for the last time. Maxwell had been my loyal companion since I was nine years old. A faithful feline who always comforted me and, in his own way supported me through my illness. A friend whom I didn't have to use as much energy to listen to as with a human, just needing enough energy to listen to his affectionate purring. We planned to look for a kitten the next spring but, as it turned out, thinking of giving a new home to a furry bundle of fun became the last thing on our minds.

CHAPTER SIXTEEN

On 23 December, 1992 I awoke to find my dad unwell. It seemed to be the start of 'flu but he was unusually vague and throughout the day his memory seemed to be failing him. My mum was worried, but I thought he was just overtired and carried out my normal activities. By the evening mum was extremely anxious, dad couldn't remember fairly simple things and seemed confused about other aspects of ordinary tasks. I too was now very concerned. My mum wanted to phone our GP but dad, as always, was reluctant to bother his former colleague.

That night I phoned Kim about dad's condition, he said it was possible that he had had a slight stroke. I was stunned. After a sleepless night dad had deteriorated. The next day our GP visited and confirmed Kim's suspicion. Dad didn't remember the doctor's name; one he had known for about 30 years having been a former colleague. He was sent immediately for a brain scan. My brother Ian took him and my mum to the hospital while I waited at home. Trying to rest wasn't easy, trembling with fear and exhaustion.

Dad returned home that afternoon, Christmas Eve. He had had a minor stroke, losing his memory and ability to sort out words in his brain, making him unable to put together a sentence with the correct words. The prognosis was good, with time he would, should, regain his abilities. I had naturally focused all my energies on my dad and that night many of my old symptoms started to appear, but I fought them physically and emotionally, I had to for my dad's sake, and my mum, she needed my support more than ever before.

Christmas was traumatic but we got through it. My passion to do anything to help dad had somehow released a new energy in me. He had become, there is no other way to describe it, 'child-like' in some of his manner. I instinctively became a nurse for him, overnight reversing the role he had been to me for the past six years.

On Christmas Day he sat quietly as we opened our presents, bemused at the names on the parcels and whom they were from. He tired so easily and was obviously distraught, as he didn't understand what was wrong with him, why he didn't understand or remember things. It was devastating to see such an intelligent man, the dad I knew and loved, behaving in this way.

In some ways my strength began to increase, I had to do more around the house to help, still being careful not to overdo things. Thankfully dad's speech began to improve quickly, his sentences became clearer as he remembered vocabulary. I began to incorporate my usual activities with the added ones of helping to care for dad. During February he became well enough to drive short distances accompanied by someone and I found an important and unforgettable new bond with him, able to talk to him about my experiences of severe illness and to try to help him regain his strength slowly. He still had difficulty in understanding why he suffered from fatigue so badly. We had some lengthy discussions about his recovery comparing it to mine and he valued my advice. I felt in my heart that we were becoming closer than we ever had been, I could at last give something back to him after all the valuable things, experiences, he had given me in my 27 years. At that point in my life, having M.E was actually of great value to me. One thing I found remarkable even when he was very ill in the first few days was that, even with his memory not functioning properly, he remembered how ill I had been, and still was. An example of this happened just three days after his stroke. Dad was resting upstairs; I was having lunch downstairs talking to mum. Shortly afterwards she took something up to him and, although he was feeling extremely unwell, with a little help from pointing actions he said to her, 'Is that Katie having lunch downstairs?' Somewhere in his memory he immediately became aware that I had never managed this before as I normally had my lunch much earlier than my family, needing to rest by the time they had theirs. It had been a big step forward for me and dad was aware of it, it was fantastic.

My progress continued, I was active every day,

walking one to one and a half miles three times a week and driving almost to the centre of Oxford once a week. Excited at my progress, dad was thrilled for me too, especially towards the end of March when I managed to drive to the centre of Oxford and walk to the first few shops. This was a major achievement for me. It had been a quiet Sunday morning, I smiled to myself staring at the beauty of the colleges as cyclists pedalled to and fro. The last time I had seen the centre of the city was in the Inspector Morse TV programmes. As I retraced my footsteps back to the car my muscles ached, I shivered from fatigue. On returning home I fell asleep for a couple of hours. Even after sleep I was still drained of energy and pale as a ghost.

After a few quiet days, I was soon to be given one of the most difficult experiences of my life to cope with.

On Saturday 27 March I arose as usual, it was a misty day but I needed some exercise and went for a long walk in Blenheim Park, just a mile from home. Dad seemed very active and keen to go out, he drove mum into Oxford to go to Blackwell's bookshop. Back at home he was fidgety and after lunch did a little gardening. I awoke from a deep two-hour sleep to find dad with a terrible headache, he was bumping into things and eventually went to lie down. The next few hours and days were too traumatic to go into in detail and unnecessary for the reader, but dad suddenly had a massive cerebral haemorrhage. He had two brain operations and two heart attacks over the next five days. His sheer strength of character kept him from slipping away, but he was in no state to live. On Wednesday 31 March dad passed away.

My sister Sue had taken the first flight home from New Zealand the moment she knew that dad had been admitted to hospital, she arrived to see him in intensive care two days before he left us. I believe he hung on especially for her. The funeral took place the following week. The church was full, almost two hundred friends and colleagues attended. For a few days prior to this I had a major relapse. I could barely walk at all and stayed in bed for the majority of the day. I gathered every ounce of strength in me to cope with laying him to rest. I felt empty, numb, and so alone. I cried a little, but the real tears came a few months later.

During the next few weeks and months my time and energy was spent consoling and comforting my mum as best as I could. I felt at my best when walking, needing to be alone with my thoughts. Having sudden outbursts of tears, letting go of the deep sadness in me. It took a good two months for me to begin to feel my strength come back. I'd lost half a stone in weight, life continued in a daze.

Summer came early, the warmth helped to rejuvenate me and by the beginning of July I managed to drive to Oxford, parked, then walked further than I'd done for years. I became an Auntie again. My brother Ian now had a son, Matthew. One of my closest friends had given birth to a girl the previous week and my best friend was due in six months, I felt very left out. One thing I wanted most in life, apart from my health returning, was to have children. At times I longed for them but then felt very disheartened because I couldn't see a time in the near future when this would be possible. Would I ever have the stamina to care for them? I still had to find a potential husband, and who would want a wife with M.E? This may sound very pessimistic but it's how I felt, it really got me down. During August the sunshine lifted my spirits a little, I had to keep hoping better times were ahead.

CHAPTER SEVENTEEN

Towards the end of the year increasing frustration took hold of me. Kim had wanted me to see an acupuncturist in Oxford for some time, but I hadn't been fit enough to go and see her. By January, having been driven to her house, I waited a little anxiously to be seen. Kim was there to introduce me and to see how I responded to my first treatment. Needles were no problem for me, they were so fine caused no pain at all. I liked Dr C straight away; she had many years of experience in Western and Chinese medicine. I felt calmed by her and was convinced she could help me.

Lethargy hit me when I returned home but my mum noticed a bright, almost cleansing, clarity in my eyes. Something had happened during the acupuncture that made her see a glimmer of wellbeing returning to me.

To begin with two or three visits were made every week to Dr C. It took about three months to begin to see a real change for the better. I had almost given up at one stage but persevered because no one else could offer me help. I was also given Chinese herbal medicine that helped to reduce the heat I suffered from in most of my muscles. The trips to Oxford exhausted me and usually sleep came easily shortly after returning home, but I was becoming a bit stronger and brighter in myself, looking forward to a future.

Physical fitness had always been strictly limited to short and very short walks. Over time, my energy had improved, acupuncture helping a great deal. I tentatively began swimming, surprisingly managing three lengths of a twenty-five-metre pool once a week and, after six months, eight lengths twice a week. An hour after getting home I'd always be sound asleep for two to three hours and feel heavy and exhausted for the rest of the day unable to do anything else but rest. The tiredness seemed worth it to achieve this physical challenge. The last time an expanse of warm water had surrounded me was nine years earlier swimming in the sea in New Zealand by a deserted beach. The local pool wasn't quite the same, but I was thrilled at my achievement nonetheless.

With physical strength slowly improving, I strongly needed mental stimulation and felt ready to look for a very part-time job to see how I could manage. Flicking through a careers book, reading about the work of a veterinary nurse inspired me. I had always had a great love for all animals but wasn't sure whether that love would see me through the more gruesome aspects of the job!

I wrote to some of the local vets inquiring about voluntary or part-time work. I was now convinced that working at a vet's was the right career path for me. Most replies were negative, without being pessimistic that was what I had expected, until Friday 13th January 1995, when I was given the lucky break I needed and deserved.

I had a phone call from one of the veterinary surgeries six miles away. My mum took the message that I could attend one of their surgeries that evening and when she told me I was stunned, suddenly filled with nerves and fear. For the next seven hours I tried to rest, I couldn't eat. The surgery was only one and a half hours long, but I was concerned whether I would manage to stand that length of time and cope with meeting new people in a working environment.

I drove anxiously along the country roads on a cold winter's day, aware that I didn't look my healthiest and that I certainly didn't feel at my best. For one and a half hours I stood and listened in the consulting room to Steve, the vet, as he went about his work, my mind wandering from time to time. The clients were friendly and the patients more so, well most of them!

After the last patient had gone Steve had time to talk. I explained about my position fearful that mentioning M.E would dissuade him from wanting me there. He explained he had a close friend with M.E and understood how little I could do, he suggested I could do some voluntary work. I was determined to prove I was capable of doing something. He would give me a chance and see how interested I really was in veterinary nursing; I should return the following Friday at 4.00 p.m. to assist the receptionist with odd light duties before surgery started and stay until 6.00 p.m.

I raced home pushing myself through mental and physical exhaustion. As my key turned in the front door mum opened it for me. Pale and weary, but my eyes beaming I said "I've got a job, well sort of". My patient and loving carer was over the moon as I began to recount my evening at the surgery but after ten minutes exhaustion overcame me and tired tears trickled down my face. Staggering up the stairs to bed, my leg muscles ached. I flopped under my welcoming duvet.

It took me a complete week to recover, resting almost completely except for one excursion up to the village shops. I slept in the afternoons and worried about the muscular pain I had but I knew I could push through it.

After five Friday evening surgeries I began to settle in, a little less tired each week and not so washed out in between. Two months into my new job I tried jumping from one session to three, my enthusiasm getting the better of me. My legs couldn't cope and for two days I could barely walk and regrettably had to cancel the following week's surgery. I didn't want Steve to think I wasn't capable of the work, but he was very understanding. One month later I was fit enough to start a second evening. I thoroughly enjoyed my time there, meeting all sorts of people and some wonderful pets. Still needing to rest most of the week to prepare for work, I managed to fit in my usual walks and the grocery shopping.

By mid July I felt obliged to try and put in more hours at the surgery and began a third evening. Now working Monday, Wednesday, and Friday, I needed the days off in between to recover. Standing for one and a half to two hours was hard for me and drained my energy but I constantly pushed through the pain and put on a brave face. Every now and again it caught up with me having small relapses.

My life revolved around my job, working six hours a week and then resting. Towards the end of the year, I managed to do an extra couple of hours every fortnight helping Steve at a local farm with pregnancy diagnoses in cattle. I enjoyed the farm visits. (I'd spent a couple of my teen years helping out on the dairy farm in our village). The farmers always had amusing stories to tell and usually saw the funny side of things. On one visit the snow lay thinly on the ground, it was minus two degrees. I was asked to hold a needle for Steve, my numb hands dropped it. I froze, literally, afraid of the consequences of a stray needle in the straw. I couldn't find it. The farmer immediately put me at my ease; laughed and said, 'You'll be looking for a needle in a haystack!' We didn't find it, but the area of straw was removed later.

The cold weather brought the return of the muntjac deer to our garden, the pair liked to shelter behind our patio wall. Many people don't like them because of the damage they can do but my mum and I found them endearing and forgave them for eating some of the garden foliage. We watched them skipping about the garden playfully, their winter visit bringing the year to a close.

CHAPTER EIGHTEEN

1996 began quietly and uneventfully until an accident at work. Whilst helping to hold a Labrador crossbreed steady as Steve gave him an internal examination, the dog in desperation to escape my clutches whipped up his hind leg and in a flash his claw ripped across my eyelid tearing it from one side to the other. Three stitches were needed and a black eye lasted for several days. I was lucky that more severe damage had not been done to my eye, the incident reminded me of the hazards of being a veterinary nurse.

The warm rays of sun heated me gently as I sunbathed in the garden on my day off. I was concerned about my health. For several weeks I had been taking a lot of homeopathic remedies to keep me going. They helped a bit, but severe weakness kept overwhelming me. Instead of waking up every other day ready to enjoy going to work, I became anxious because I knew I wasn't fit enough. When returning home I literally collapsed in a heap with exhaustion and muscle pain, usually too tired to speak. The following is an outline of an average workday to give the reader an idea of how little I could still do after ten years of illness.

7.30 a.m. Get up, shower, breakfast, read the newspaper

8.30 a.m. Rest
9.00 - 9.30 a.m. Walk ten to twenty minutes (on a good day) 9.30 a.m. Rest
10.30 -11.30 a.m. Potter about and early lunch
11.30 a.m. Rest
1.00 p.m. Get up
1.30 p.m. Rest
3.00 - 3.15 p.m. Get ready for work
3.15 - 3.30 p.m. Rest
3.30 - 6.30 p.m. Go to work
6.30 - 7.00 p.m. Home, grab supper and straight to bed, usually collapsing exhausted, stay there until the next day.

By the end of August I had a severe relapse and was devastated to need three weeks off work. Weakness and pain swamped me, barely able to stand or walk at all. Tears rolled down my pale face daily, distraught at still suffering so much after so many years and the worry as to when and whether I'd manage to work again.

For two weeks bed rest was the only answer and then, gradually walking and standing for a few minutes around the house. Morag, the receptionist at the vets, had arranged a huge basket of flowers to be delivered to my house, it was typical of the thoughtfulness and kindness she had always shown me since my first day at the practice. The bouquet was from all the staff.

Returning to work was a real battle against fatigue and muscular weakness. The staff were so good to me, I began by coping with half an hour at a time, eventually getting back to two hours three times a week. All my free time was spent resting, by the following spring my GP again referred me to a consultant at the John Radcliffe Hospital in Oxford as my health wasn't improving. Several blood tests and a lung function test proved fruitless. Everything was normal, it always was. Sometimes, time was the only way to see improvements, often wasted time. At this point in my illness it seemed to be the only thing that gradually helped me regain strength.

Subconsciously I knew that working was too much for me but it had so many benefits, this was proven in being given the opportunity to study to become a pet health counsellor. Veterinary practices were aiming to be seen as a place to go for preventative care as well as when needing help for illness and injury. The PHC course was divided into specialist areas such as bereavement and behavioural therapy, but I specialised in clinical nutrition with emphasis on overweight pets.

My training was achieved by hourly meetings at the vets, very tiring but manageable. By the end of the year, I had set up my own obesity clinic for cats and dogs. Many people may find this amusing, but in fact weight control is just as much a serious issue for pets as for humans and can help prevent and reduce suffering from problems such as arthritis and heart disease.

My clinics became very popular, and very successful. My greatest achievement was shown with a Labrador that should on average be a healthy twenty-seven kilograms, but when Candy waddled in she was a massive fifty kilograms! Time and patience, the correct diet, continued encouragement and exercise planning rewarded Candy and her owner about a year later with a dog that had a new lease of life at thirty-three kilograms.

I gained a tremendous amount from my clinics, especially a huge dose of self-confidence. Being locked in a prison of illness for so many years, I thought my battle was slowly being won.

CHAPTER NINETEEN

My boots crushed the white tipped grass after a sharp frost, but it wouldn't take long to melt, the sun was already quite strong on this beautiful January morning. My twenty minute walk tired me but made me feel fitter and gave me just another short break from my familiar bed. I stopped to chat to a villager for a few minutes as his dog sniffed the cold air subtly drifting across the ploughed field.

Ten minutes later, lying resting I was deep in thought. My enthusiasm and enjoyment for work was a great part of my limited lifestyle, but my outlook in general seemed so bleak. I wanted to be well, to do ordinary things, more than anything in the world. Working a little, exercising a little, the rest of my life was spent resting. I cried almost every day for the next couple of months, desperate for someone or something to help give me some hope.

Still in regular contact with Kim, I rang him late one evening. After a lengthy conversation, I hurried in to my mum's room with a beaming smile and brightened eyes. Kim had met an Australian scientist who used a unique form of treatment that had helped many M.E patients in his home country. I couldn't begin to understand how the process worked, neither did Kim exactly, but we both had a 'gut' feeling that the 'ortho-homeopathic' treatment would help me significantly. Based on working with a system of meridians (energy channels) found at a cellular level, a combination of meridian theory and orthodox cellular biology that is as much as I knew and could explain. I sent a saliva swab to Chris in Australia and waited eagerly to see what his tests found.

At the beginning of April, the first report arrived. Chris had found a complex of viruses, consistent with other cases of M.E he had studied. He explained that the disease affected the pituitary gland, in turn affecting the nervous and hormonal systems, giving the diverse symptoms of M.E. The viral complex needed to be removed before the damage it had caused could be treated. The test also showed evidence of muscle pain, foggy thinking and, of course, energy deficiency.

The treatment in the form of oral drops for six days was likely to cause an immune response, exacerbating my symptoms temporarily. I would feel worse before feeling better. Symptoms appeared rapidly: weakness, muscle aches, exhaustion and very poor concentration, but this was nothing compared to the severity treatment two caused. These symptoms were so intense, they were unlike anything I had experienced for several years. The drops of medicine had made me feel as ill as I had first felt back in 1986. I was upset at suffering so much, barely able to move even in bed, resting because of such extreme weakness and feeling so unwell in myself, but I had a gut feeling that it was ok.

The drops were forcing my body to reactivate the virus remaining in me and trying to get my poor weak body to respond and heal. Reassurance from Chris and Kim helped, but it was a terrible experience to go through, I needed another three weeks off work because I was so unwell.

Gradually over the next month things improved, managing a little work, where I was given reception duties for several weeks so that I could remain seated all the time. Standing for more than five - ten minutes just caused me to collapse into a chair, but underneath all these symptoms there was some definite improvement resulting from my Australian treatment. My mental clarity, concentration and memory were noticeably better than they had been since before my illness.

Chris could clearly see from my test results, after studying my saliva each time that I had truly been severely affected by this terrible disease. He was very encouraged by my reactions. I was to try and conserve energy where and when I could, needing it to repair all the damage that had been caused by so many years severely unwell.

Towards the end of the year, after treatment five, I was encouraged by Chris's report stating that the severity of the disease had decreased by one level. Not a great deal but any improvement was better than none. I had every faith in Chris, maybe that wasn't the best thing, but I needed something to cling on to, to know someone else was really trying to help me even if it was in an unconventional way.

I still had acupuncture regularly and Dr C helped enormously. I couldn't manage without her and seemed to benefit more from that therapy when I had acute symptoms. Chris was working much more deeply at cellular level. I needed both their treatments; they worked in such different ways.

CHAPTER TWENTY

Grey skies darkened early as winter set in. With it came seasonal 'flu. Disheartened, I spent a week in bed with a fever and the other usual ailments, it took a good six weeks until I regained my lost strength. At work, staff had changed; the surgery expanded its hours and started to offer more services, the atmosphere changed completely. For the next eight months I continued my thrice-weekly hours at the vets but, very unhappily, the stress of forced pressures there sadly left me no other conclusion than to leave the practice. The stress had caused severe health problems, I felt at breaking point, so desperately weary and weak. I knew I'd made the right decision, only later did I wish I'd left sooner, to have stopped my health deteriorating so much.

I missed the good friends and wonderful clients that had made my first four years there so much fun. My life had changed for the better with my learning experience, developing many new skills and being rewarded with respect by staff and clients. I never imagined I would have enough self-belief to set up and run my own clinic. It had all been an important step in my recovery, but it became clear that, although working had great advantages for me, going to the surgery for seven and a half to nine hours a week and resting completely at all other times, it was no way to live a life or progress with my health, leaving was the right decision.

Another year was drawing to a close. Something that frequently came to mind was an intense longing and desire for a holiday. I had lived in my family home, my comfy prison, for thirteen years, day in day out. The only break in all that time was a total of eight weeks in hospital over ten years ago. I can't put into words what it felt like to be confined for so long. The furthest I had been from my home was twelve miles, I had never been away for longer than three and a half hours.

My eyes filled with tears as I relived the years of lack of independence and freedom. I couldn't remember what it felt like to experience control of what I wanted to do every day, to go about life impulsively. All I remember is thirteen long years of counting minutes, how many paces I could walk, and how many minutes I could talk to friends for, all needing bed rest soon after. A radical change was due, long, long overdue, I felt ready for it.

Sunlight filtered through a small gap in the curtains. With only a little sleep, my mind was buzzing with excitement and nerves. Most of my luggage was in the car, loaded the previous day, far too much, but what would I need? Packing bags for a holiday, it was weird and seemed unreal.

Resting all day until 3.00 p.m. I said my goodbyes to my mum. Reversing down the drive waving, holding back tears, setting off on my epic journey. An independent holiday after so long. Tears of joy, excitement, fear, worry, wondering if I'd manage or was fit enough to cope, and the sense of loss at leaving my mum at home alone. The break would be good for both of us.

My journey's end was only ten miles away to a lovely little cottage, no comparison to the twelve and a half thousand miles I'd travelled alone to New Zealand on my last holiday, aged twenty.

Forge Cottage was set in a tiny hamlet in the heart of a valley, I could have been hundreds of miles from home, not ten. Although living so close, I had never visited this area before. After a quick look around the quaint cottage and phoning my mum to let her know I was ok, my legs began to tremble, heat set in. Lying down in my bedroom, tears slowly filled my eyes. So many emotions flickered through my mind. This was a huge event for me. The overpowering emotions used a lot of nervous energy transferring themselves into M.E symptoms, a common occurrence. Immobile for three hours with intense heat in my muscles, part of me wanted to be at home so I could relax in surroundings I knew well, too well.

I've always found it hard to explain to people why I couldn't travel far, even if someone else was driving. I had so little energy that every time my eyes saw something new, not just small objects, but new rooms, houses, areas of landscape, my body would use huge amounts of it in absorbing the new sights, draining me mentally and physically. This is one of the reasons my holiday was so important to me, to see how badly I was still affected by this. Walking slowly downstairs I heated up a prepared meal in the microwave but was soon back in bed nauseous with fatigue. I phoned my mum needing reassurance and a friendly voice. She was sure I'd manage the night on my own and could bear with the symptoms. I could have packed my bags and gone home there and then but I didn't feel fit enough or capable, I wanted to prove to myself that I could manage one night on my own.

The quiet still night dragged on as I listened to each and every new sound the house made. In the morning I felt drained. Resting again after breakfast I then packed my bags, needing to go home. It had all been traumatic if beneficial for me. Arriving home in tears, feeling as though I'd let myself down at not coping better, my mum consoled me 'You have managed Katie, you've managed a night away on your own after all these years, it's a wonderful thing, it's a start'.

After three days of rest and sleep I returned to my little cottage (as it had been rented for the week) and stayed another day and night coping better, more relaxed and realising the huge achievement that had been made.

CHAPTER TWENTY - ONE

Treatment twelve arrived from Australia at the beginning of November. Chris had been waiting for a lift in my energy, but this wasn't happening. He reminded me of how truly a very frustrating disease M.E is not only to suffer from but also to treat and advised me to try and keep focusing on the positive aspects such as improvements in mental clarity. The last swab sample showed my general system was continuing to improve. I took the drops as usual.

At this time, I was also struggling to cope with my mum's health. She had been unwell on and off for the past four years but no definite diagnosis had been made. After many visits to her GP, an angiogram was arranged for the end of January 2000. This procedure looks at the arteries leading to the heart and can detect any problems.

For the three months prior to this test my mum deteriorated so much that every night when I went to bed I seriously wondered if she would be alive the next morning. The reader will appreciate this put tremendous pressure on me and pulled my energy down considerably but of course I was far more concerned about my mum than myself.

The worry and stress was too much, I was finding it difficult to cope. My mum agreed a break for a few days would do me good. I booked a cottage nearby again and managed a couple of days and nights on my own having first promised that I would be home in a flash if mum needed me. My brothers were also ready to come home and look after her if necessary.

On my return I was horrified at how unwell my frail mum looked and felt guilty for having been away although she said she'd been ok. The next day she had the angiogram and spent the whole day at the John Radcliffe Hospital in Oxford. My brother Ian brought her home at 7.00 p.m. She looked pale and exhausted. Sitting on a hall chair, with me on the stairs close by she told me the terrible news. She needed a coronary triple bypass. The words hit me like a ton of bricks. For the next few days, we talked about the operation, our worries and fears. The angiogram procedure had taken a lot out of her fragile body, she deteriorated rapidly, daily.

A week after the test she collapsed on my bed after breakfast. I called her GP immediately; he came out straight away and called an ambulance. The paramedics wanted to carry her downstairs, but she insisted she try and walk. Her GP told me quietly that I needed to be brave, I tried but was scared. She settled in the ambulance, I wasn't well enough to go to the hospital with her, and shouted, 'You'll be ok mum'. She quietly said, 'Go inside, it's too cold'. My dearest mum looked so unwell, a sudden fear swamped me, I might never see her again. The last time an ambulance came into our drive they had taken my dad away; he never came home.

Ten days later a very frail, exceptionally pale lady arrived home, five days after an emergency double coronary bypass. The surgeon had planned to operate on a third artery but didn't find this feasible. The operation had saved her life.

The following month passed somehow, a tremendous struggle. My mum was obviously low and weak from open heart surgery and was trying to regain her strength, I could barely walk at times I had so little energy. Both my brothers helped tremendously when they could, but getting time off work wasn't easy and they had their own families to care for. Friends and neighbours were great helping with shopping needs.

Two weeks later my sister Sue was able to come over from New Zealand. She had been desperate to come earlier to be there for mum but work and family commitments had made that difficult for her. Sue had a busy fortnight, taking mum for short rides in the car, taking her to appointments and lifting her spirits. It was a tremendous weight off my shoulders to have someone else around to take responsibility. I picked up, and by the time Sue left there, was a little more energy in the house.

By May, treatment fourteen had arrived from Australia, its effect this time was to send me to sleep day and night almost constantly for one month. I didn't feel at all unwell, just slept, letting my body unwind and recover from the traumas of the past six months.

Over the summer I continued to improve, mum's recovery was slow with added complications post-surgery, which was very disheartening for her. Coronary bypasses are so common nowadays and most people make a speedy recovery, mum was unlucky.

My energy slowly started to flow. Walking fifteen minutes every other day, not a great deal but not bad, and driving for half an hour's shopping, not falling asleep for hours once returning home. Life was beginning to change. My swab results from Australia were encouraging; I was on the verge of a breakthrough. After fourteen years of ill health, I was at my best yet, then disaster struck, a family row destroyed the next eighteen months of my life.

CHAPTER TWENTY - TWO

My body was completely drained, emotionally, physically, and psychologically. I was terribly unwell. The worst part was not that I was again physically capable of doing so little and in a lot of muscular pain, but the psychological damage that had been caused. Spending the previous two years gaining confidence in myself feeling I really was making progress, that the worst was over, I would never be so unwell (with M.E) again. My life was now in pieces, losing so much energy I was barely able to function.

For the next eighteen months I battled daily to recover my lost physical and emotional strength. Energy just didn't want to return, a couple of times I reached complete despair and just wanted to give up. My mum gave me so much support and understanding, I couldn't have managed without her. My days consisted of two to three minute walks around the garden, driving to the village shops and spending hours resting. It had been the wettest winter on record, the heavy dull days didn't inspire my mood.

The latest report from Australia had fantastic news, my swab sample showed no signs of viral remnants. For the first time in fifteen years, I was clear of viruses. There were though, still problems in trying to get my cells to generate energy, not only to help heal but also to give me energy to be well and active again. This was a huge step forward. Although I still obviously had a very restricted lifestyle my body really was healing, deep down.

Shades of red and brown crept across the green leaves of summer; autumn was on its way. My energy levels had improved a little with Chris's treatment but at best my day revolved around walking once or twice for eight minutes, no more. One minute more would almost double the fatigue I felt whilst trying to recoup the energy just used. Rest still consumed my days.

Leading up to Christmas my mood became very despondent. Sitting gazing out of the frosty window across the barren fields, tears rolled quickly down my cheeks; my eyes became red and puffy with days of crying. I've written about the despair I've felt on many occasions throughout this long drawn out illness of mine, but the longer it continued the harder it became to fight. Sadly it was always clear to me why some people decide to give up the battle with M.E. I had come very close to that point, but somehow underlying determination to be well was so strong, I'm not sure where that came from. I've always managed to see myself as being well again. After fifteen years that's an exceptionally hard thing to hang on to. Through daily tears I had to cling to the hope that 2002 would be the year that I let go of chronic fatigue.

CHAPTER TWENTY - THREE

January began with some ground-breaking news for all M.E sufferers and their carers'. A report commissioned by the government stated that doctors must recognise chronic fatigue syndrome as a serious illness, and a greater understanding of the illness was needed in the medical profession. Doctors and nurses should be taught about it in their training.

The government's Chief Medical Office, Sir Liam Donaldson, said that 'Until now on the whole sufferers have been ignored, not always taken seriously, sometimes labelled hypochondriacs, urged to pull themselves together and get better on their own. From today that changes'.

Taking a deep breath, I tried to calm myself as deep emotions and memories flooded back, memories of all my suffering that could have been reduced or avoided altogether, if only this report had been put together years before. A while later the importance of this really sunk in. It was a huge step forward and only good would come out of it for those suffering now and in the future.

During February my dark mood was temporarily lifted one evening when the security light outside my bedroom lit the garden below. Carefully drawing back a curtain I smiled at the rare sight before me and shouted for my mum to come and look. The female muntjac deer that had visited us on many occasions during the past nine years had her head down over a plate full of seeds that I left out for the birds, she was licking them with her very long tongue. Standing delicately beside her was her fawn. It couldn't have been more than four to six weeks old. This adorable little creature was no larger than a small cat. I had never seen a fawn before, and watching it with its mother, my mum and I felt privileged to see such wildlife on our doorstep.

July was to become one of my most memorable times throughout my illness. It started with treatment twenty-nine from Australia, arriving with a report to say that my cells were starting to generate energy. I began to take vitamin B complex with minerals. This supplement turned my life around.

My immediate reaction was severe depression for a week, (an uncommon reaction) then one day I awoke feeling entirely different. My whole body felt as though it was trying to renew itself, that may sound odd, but it seems a good way to describe my sensations. Fourteen days after starting the vitamin B complex I found myself rummaging around the garage looking for a bicycle pump. My bike hadn't been ridden for about eighteen years.

With a huge smile, straddled the seat and cautiously began to pedal once around the garden. The exercise was hard for my thigh muscles. They really ached! It was a normal unused ache not an M.E ache. I found a new lease of life in this activity and for the next three months it almost took over my life. Making an exercise program with very small increments for walking distances as well as cycling, I began to make a tremendous leap forward in my recovery. After ten weeks of going around the garden and then progressing with confidence to cycling on the road, I achieved my target of FOUR miles! It was almost impossible to believe! At this point I was certain M.E had gone. I decided I no longer needed to label myself as having M.E, I was recovering from it. I couldn't have achieved these distances if I still had M.E and, instead of the exercise making me tired it was actually giving me energy and also allowing me to reduce my rest times. As I reached a five mile target (one at which I was going to remain for some time while trying to and achieve that distance more frequently) 'flu arrived and stopped me in my tracks.

CHAPTER TWENTY - FOUR

Recovery from the 'flu took several weeks. During that time, I began to read more than I had been able to for years, some easy-going novels, but also understandings of the psychology and consciousness associated with aspects of illness, healing and moving on in life when you have been blocked in some way. These were a little heavy going in places, but it only confirmed that my mental abilities of learning and concentration had improved dramatically. It was towards the end of February 2003 that I finally got back on track with my exercise and again started reaching five miles when cycling.

One of my greatest hurdles was yet to come. Moving home. At age thirty-seven I was long overdue more independence and growth in my life, to live on my own, away from the nurturing family home. My mum and I had discussed the idea over several months. I felt completely ready and able to try and achieve my goal. With help from Housing Benefit entitlement and financial help from my mum, on 24th March I moved into a lovely little rented cottage on the edge of a village green just on the outskirts of our local market town. As soon as I stepped over the front door I felt totally at home, at ease and very happy.

My new life began with not as much energy as I'd hoped. Due to the international problem of the S.A.R.S. virus, the saliva sample I sent to Australia kept getting held up in quarantine, by the time it reached Chris, weeks after its departure from England, it was out of date and no use for testing. The process was repeated three times until four months later I could proceed with the treatment that helped me so much.

Although my life was still very restricted, I sometimes found it hard to remember just how unwell I had been and that now, although it had taken over sixteen years I was not just coping, but successfully managing to look after myself and take on the responsibilities needed to run a home. These few months were vitally important to me; I made new friends and gained a great deal of self-belief and confidence, mentally stronger if not physically.

In early January 2004 I had to leave my little cottage and return to live with my mum. It had become too expensive to continue my independence. After a glimpse of freedom living on my own and looking after my cottage, returning to my mum's was extremely hard. She said I'd definitely changed for the better and when asking her in what way she replied, 'it may sound odd but I think you're more grown up.' I didn't know quite how to take that at first because I was thirty-eight years old, I should already be 'grown up', but so many years of ill health had held me back from achieving normal goals in life that help adults achieve maturity.

I felt trapped at my mum's, going back to a house

which had seventeen years of illness in it and a 'heaviness' that went with that. My friend Annemarie had told me 'You are going back a different person.' I tried hard to acknowledge this and not let the new me slip away.

I became extremely despondent. Although I still desperately wanted to be well to begin my life I had lost the strong incentive to want to be better because I was so tired of fighting for it. Chris was continuing to work hard at aiding my recovery. I was still having difficulty in producing energy in my cells and he believed that the problem was at a fundamental level of energy production. Every cell in the body (except red blood cells and the lens of the eye) has a few hundred mitochondria, (the power in cells) each produce a substance called adenosine triphosphate (ATP). When muscles are used the ATP is broken down into adenosine diphosphate and inorganic phosphate, this process produces cellular energy.

Another bout of flu pushed my emotions to the lowest level. I couldn't see any point in continuing my life, seriously wanting to end it. Every time, and I mean every time for seventeen and a half years that I began to make progress something halted me in my tracks. I couldn't take many more relapses, on top of that I found myself getting cross and upset with people for having to fight to prove my utmost determination to be well. Others thought they knew best, knew what's right for me, (they had no idea) they were forceful with their opinions, wouldn't listen to me. I was just trying to find my place back in this world after years of 'being away'.

I didn't have the energy to fight my corner and I shouldn't have had to; I was trying to be a well woman again with every ounce of energy I had. Why wouldn't people listen to me? It hurt so deeply.

Every word that I write in this book goes someway to explain the destruction M.E had caused me, but the words you read are really only a summary, you would have to have been my mum or dad to have seen the daily on going battles I fought, physically but probably more importantly emotionally.

Chris's next report lifted my spirits enormously. He had new equipment that could 'see' even deeper into cells than previous testing, he found something very interesting; there were still signs of Glandular Fever that hadn't been completely cleared by my immune system. He had suspected this but never been able to find it before. This excited him, Kim and me because it could be the answer to why I had taken so very long to recover and why some of the treatments I'd tried had not worked or made my symptoms much worse. I then started Chris's next course of drops; these too were to help bring out the hidden Glandular Fever remnants but working at a much deeper level than homeopathy.

The rest of that year continued remaining at a stable but low rate of energy. Chris's medicine swayed from bringing out symptoms to helping me progress slowly. As the year drew to a close I thought of one achievement I'd made in 2004, In the spring I'd begun a computer course (studying at home) and had managed with difficulty because of fatigue, to go to a local school at intervals over six months to take seven, forty-five minute exams. Just before Christmas I completed and passed my final exam. I was proud of myself.

CHAPTER TWENTY - FIVE

The year 2005 became one of great change in many directions. I joined an evening class in Archery, a big step forward for me to join a group activity and go out in the evening, something I just didn't do as I was usually too tired to go out then. Walking into the sports hall of a local school, for a moment I felt I'd entered into a time warp, the smell (not odour!) of the hall and the sounds underfoot from trainers took me back to my days at school when I'd been so fit and well. I was quietly overwhelmed at the experience to feel 'normal' in a gym playing a sport even though the energy level needed was significantly lower than for a racquet or ball game. My hourly lessons over 10 weeks exhausted me, but I gained a tremendous amount from it, confidence in talking to new people, having fun, which is something my life lacked and finding out that I was actually quite good at the sport! I joined for a second term. Even though I gained obvious benefits it came to the point I felt it was wasting too much of my week needing so much rest, I couldn't be too active the day of the class in order to have the energy to go to it, the day or two after spending most of the time asleep or needing total rest, so reluctantly gave up.

Thursday 21 July, I sat reading the morning paper at breakfast and couldn't quite believe a headline, 'M.E is in the genes not in the mind, say scientists.

I couldn't read on fast enough. A team led by Dr Jonathan Kerr, from Imperial College London had made a breakthrough in research which could lead to a blood test for the disorder and drugs to treat it. The research showed clear physical changes in fatigue syndrome sufferers. Dr Kerr's team discovered that sufferers white blood cells behaved differently from the cells of non-sufferers, several cell genes seemed to show that there was a continuing viral infection causing the condition. Russell Lane a neurologist at Charing Cross Hospital in London said 'This exciting new work shows that some aspects of this complex illness may be understandable in molecular terms and that chronic fatigue syndrome is not a made up illness'

Dr Charles Shepherd a medical adviser to the M.E Association said 'This work is very significant. It gives us clues about genetic abnormalities that can guide new research into the causal mechanism of the condition, which hopefully can lead us to novel treatments.'

The third time I read the article, my eyes filled with tears, I'd been waiting 18 and a half years for this news. Not only did it emphasize again to any non believer that the condition does exist, but that most importantly a real diagnoses and a cure could be on its way. This was truly remarkable to read. I'd spent over 18 years fighting my own battles to try and be well, persevered every single day to fight this disease, I never had a break from it, every day was a battle. Now, maybe there was real hope for a faster and full recovery using drugs to speed up this process. In the meantime more research had to be carried out, I presumed it could be quite some time before any 'cure' was actually available.

For the previous two years my mum and I had discussed on many occasions the prospect of moving to downsize from our quite large four bed roomed home, but my mum was very keen to stay in the road where we were as she has been there for just over fifty years (our last move in 1970 just next door) I had been still far too unwell to think of trying to move before now. An old bungalow just six houses along from us had been knocked down the previous autumn, two semi-detached cottage style houses were being built in its place. We bought one. For ten months we trekked up and down the road seeing the cottage rise up and thanks to the builder we had great input in most aspects of the internal fixtures, floors, bathroom, kitchen, down to the smallest detail. In between my bouts of small relapses mum and I went shopping for all the necessities which was extremely tiring but fun. I became deeply involved with the project, it consumed me, but to my great relief I managed with very little setbacks, my physical energy levels held up well, and most noticeably my mental abilities were challenged more so than they had been since I had first become unwell, but I actually found almost all the problems straightforward and it bought out my organisational skills that I hadn't used to my fullest since my school days, it was a huge step forward in moving on with my life in many ways.

Moving was traumatic but for unexpected reasons. Mid September, five days before the move my mum was rushed to hospital with severe angina, frightening both of us at one of the most stressful times of any one's life. Although still very unwell, mum was discharged late the night before the move. We had exceptionally thoughtful removal men who were understanding of our situation and had been around a couple of days earlier to help move two bedrooms worth of furniture so that mum and myself could go straight to bed when the main move began, it made a world of difference to the whole day but even so we both deteriorated and spent most of the next 6 weeks needing a lot of bed rest.

It was one of the coldest prolonged winters, we made great use of our new wood burning stove whiling away some time watching the glowing flames and piling on the logs. The cottage was cosy and beautiful, after nineteen years 'cooped' up in our old house with so much of my past illness surrounding me, living in a different property with a different soul and ambiance gave me a new lease of life, in some respects.

It began to sink in; everything that I had achieved

during the past year, taking control of all aspects of leaving a family home after thirty-five years, clearing it physically and mentally and at the same time building a new home and sorting out all the finances. It was clear my mental abilities were far stronger, my physical strength just needed to catch up.

Downsizing had released some capital from our old family home, one of the reasons for the move was to enable me to buy an apartment, to really help me begin a new life independently. I was teetering on my fortieth birthday and was still living with my mum. I know it is a common occurrence nowadays for people to move back with their parents because of financial instability, divorce etc, with the price of property so high, but the difference being that I had never been way, never lived with my friends, shared a home, or been married.

In November 2005 I began to seriously look for an apartment locally. It wasn't easy on my budget; I live in one of the most expensive areas of the country. It took four months of endless searching to finally find a one bed apartment in a local market town seven miles from my mum. I began the process for a purchasing a property. Buying 'off plan', I naturally became more involved in the development which I enjoyed but half way through realised I hadn't fully recovered from the first move only six months previously, and wondered if I could cope with the whole process again, but I had little choice, if I didn't follow through with this purchase it could take months to find something else I could afford and through previous experience my relationship with my mum may have suffered, being on top of each other '24/7' month after month if I'd stayed with her and had no prospect of my own home to look forward to.

Six weeks before my move, I achieved something amazing and unbelievable. For my fortieth birthday I had always wanted to do something special, after all it was traditional, and as I had missed out on so many birthdays where I should have been well enough to enjoy myself I had always hoped that this 'big one' would be special and one to remember.

Flicking through a magazine at special gift days my eye was struck by one advert that I thought was just about within my capabilities, well almost if slightly mad for someone who had been so unwell for so long. A trial flight lesson! The main reason this caught my attention was that I live only ten minutes from one of Britain's best known flight training schools, so the journey there and back would be no problem, (all the other gift days were just that, days out, I couldn't manage that) the actual lesson was only 30 minutes long, that seemed possible for my limitations. Further investigation made me determined to try it and suffer the consequences afterwards. During a fairly stable phase of energy levels and after reading quite a lengthy book on 'Your introductory trial flight', I found myself making a phone call to the airport and booking a lesson for the next day, it left me little time to think about how crazy and bizarre this idea was! This challenge was so important to me, if the reader thinks back to almost twenty years with no holiday and no escape from my local surroundings, trapped within a small radius of my village.

It was certainly a small plane. (For any experts a Piper Cherokee 140) Seated tightly beside the young confident pilot our thighs almost touching I listened on my headphones to the conversation between the pilot and air traffic control. Strange memories flittered through my head, the type of conversation and tone of voice that is only heard from a pilot, millions of people hear this every day whilst travelling by plane, but for me it was just a memory from so long ago, now that memory was alive again. Looking across at Paul the pilot wearing his sunglasses, I slipped mine on, it wasn't particularly sunny, but I thought it would look 'cool' as I wasn't in the passenger seat but the 'pilot in command' seat!

Shortly after a quick take off Paul flew over my village and descended low over our house so I could take photos. I felt as though I was dreaming, in such a different environment and state of mind, being far from the ground. (Between 500 and 2000 feet) With Paul's instruction I took the controls tentatively but confidently. I was now flying all on my own. The freedom was immense, totally exhilarating and really beyond belief when thoughts flickered through my mind of the torturous process I'd been through to arrive at this point. The thirty minutes was over before I knew it. After a smooth landing I climbed out of the aircraft buzzing with exhilaration. Returning home with a certificate of 'experience' I stayed on a 'high' for a couple of hours going over and over in my mind the experience of a life time.

By mid-afternoon I had heat in all my muscles again, an old symptom, I was shaking with exhaustion. Soon after I fell asleep, apart from struggling to get up for meals slept most of the next four days and nights. It took about ten days to feel back to the way I had before my flight, this really pleased me, I thought it would have taken longer to recover.

I loved the whole experience so much I decided I wanted to become a pilot! The downside being the expense for the training but also I would have to be really well to be able to deal with the stresses and time involved. I felt it could be one of very few things that could help me almost 'wipe out' all my years of ill health if I could come out of it with something quite extraordinary as having a private pilot's licence. Maybe one day?!

I had a lovely email from Chris and his wife Lyn in Australia in reply to recounting my flying lesson saying I should be very proud of myself and that it showed how close I was to a full recovery. Those words meant so much to me.

During the first week in June, I moved into my small apartment, my own home at last. The move was straight forward except I had caught a nasty viral bug two weeks before so was more tired than I should have been, but my friend Sally and her daughters helped me. Set on a brand new development to be completed the following Spring I was only the second person to occupy a residence, so it was very quiet when the workmen left at the end of the day. I liked that.

Three weeks after moving my sister Sue and nephew Alex came over from New Zealand to stay with my mum for a fortnight, so I moved back with them in order to see more of my family. We had a wonderful time the weather was the hottest on record for July. I joined them for short walks, and played croquet in the back garden, that became a daily challenge. I won the first game but neither Sue nor I could catch up with Alex's continual winning streak! I was able to do more with them than I had for many years, Sue noticed a big difference in my health.

Things were generally going well, but as always I wished my recovery would speed up. For several months I had been keeping my eye open for part time jobs, I needed to and wanted to work but I knew that I could only manage two or three hours a couple of times a week, it proved exceptionally hard to find something for those few hours. I checked ten websites daily for local work, looked at local notice boards, asked everyone I knew and looked into voluntary work just to get me started on the routine of working again but it seemed a fruitless task. I applied for two jobs but am sure my health played a major factor in my negative responses.

With a stronger and progressive year coming to a close, the last three months of 2006 were hard going. I caught yet another 'flu – like bug which took weeks to fully recover, the continual damp winter months plagued my sinusitis problems keeping my energy and self-esteem very low. At the same time my mums' health was very poor.

The year 2007 got off to a bad start with her having a suspected small stroke during the first week of January. I spent much of my time with my mum doing my best to help emotionally and practically. My brothers came over when they could with groceries and stayed a night or two to give me a break but worrying about and caring for her naturally drained more energy.

By April a brief change in the weather brought a warm dry spell, this lifted mine and my mums energy and spirits a little. A long phone call with my closest friend Annemarie also helped pull me out of a black hole I found myself sliding into.

She said, "There is a difference in your voice now, yes you sound 'flat' as a 'low' person and you have every reason, but it's not an 'ill' low depressed voice and that's something I haven't been able to say to you for 20 years. It's a credit to you how you have come through such a devastating illness as far as you have, so strong in yourself as a person, others wouldn't."

That touched me. Its words like that from people closest to me that have helped me not only keep going but literally survive.

I perused a list of main goals that I had written many years ago.

1) Work full time
2) Holiday abroad
3) Stay with friends who live an hour or so away
4) Drive 1 – 2 hours
5) Be out of bed all day
6) Have a family of my own

Goal number two had been a dream for so long, not only to go abroad but to have some time away from my surroundings I knew far too well. A real break, not just a few miles up the road as I had managed a few years before. Most people have a couple of holidays a year, whether they are able to go abroad or just holiday in the UK. Many others have weekend's away, travel around the country to see relatives and friends even just for a day out. Many say, 'Oh, I need a holiday!' Yes many people work very hard, need and deserve a holiday, but I don't think many people can imagine what it's like to have 'needed' a holiday for 20 years.

Number six was the goal that haunted me the most. I'm not an overly ambitious person, all I have ever wanted from life is to be healthy and have children. I felt I'd been put on this planet for a reason it was to be a loving, giving, devoted nurturing mother. Now 41 years old and seemingly yet so far from being able to achieve my burning desire, it constantly tortured my soul as my biological clock ticked away.

CHAPTER TWENTY - SIX

Excitedly walking on a layer of sandy pathway, I was in a totally different world. My beaming eyes darted around everywhere, digital camera in hand. One of my smaller goals for about 15 years was to visit my local Wildlife Park, only eight and a half miles from my apartment. It had always been too much of a challenge for me to tackle as there is a fair bit of walking to do (although it is a small park compared to many around the country) in addition to the drive there and back. I'd been waiting for the warmer, dryer weather to venture into this new activity.

Nearing the penguin enclosure, I smelt the sea; it seemed so abnormal compared to my daily life to watch the humorous creatures darting around the water, diving in and leaping out. Walking around the park, my legs carried me easily, egging me on to the larger animals. Zebras and Rhinos seemed so bizarre to witness just a few miles from my home, it was hard to absorb. I felt like a small child seeing these creatures for the very first time. Mentally I picked out a point at the end of the trail I was heading down to stop and turn around before I tired too much, but as I reached a bushy corner past the camels, was stopped in my tracks with the deep bellowing roar of a lion, it sounded so near, it was, just behind the bushes, in its enclosure of course! I stood in awe of this magnificent beast standing proudly, high on a wooden framework facing me, calling for his mate. Reluctantly strolling back to the car, I had to give in to my oncoming fatigue.

It may not be on quite a par with the flying lesson the previous year, but my forty-five minutes observing animals that belong all around the world thrilled me. A lifelong dream would be to see some of them in their natural habitat.

One important, positive change that had taken place during the past eighteen months in particular, was an increase in weight. I'm sure the majority of women reading this would be horrified to think it was a benefit! At the peak severity of my illness, I was only 5st 12lbs, I had spent many years trying desperately to gain weight having been insulted by doctors who declared I was anorexic; it couldn't have been further from the truth. Now I was a healthy 8st 4lbs, at 5ft 1in and a very fortunate genetically slim frame, finding for the first time in my life that I was just a little aware of my weight gain and didn't want to be any heavier feeling comfortable as I was. Whether the weight was due to progressive healing or just signs of getting older and reaching middle age spread! I don't know but it was one thing less in my battle for recovery to worry about. My body portrayed me as a very healthy looking woman.

Rain, rain, go away come again another day. Torrential downpours swept the south west of Britain in just a few hours. It didn't occur to me how bad things were at first until the following day. Returning to the market town where I lived late afternoon, as I neared the bottom of the hill just half a mile from my flat I couldn't believe my eyes when a river greeted me instead of the road. Emergency services scattered all around redirecting me away from the scene. I was already very tired but having to find an alternative route home an extra four miles drive, my legs felt noticeably wearier, by the time I reached my flat I headed straight to bed. Within a few hours the local river had burst its banks and the main route out of town was shut. Several roads became a scene of disaster, but thankfully I was not directly affected by any of the flooding. Watching many of the TV news bulletins the scenes in my neighbouring county Gloucestershire were horrific, the worst in British history.

During the following week, driving along the main street out of town I felt moved seeing piles of soiled, ruined furniture, people's lifelong possessions piled neatly and carefully on the pavements outside their devastated homes. Sandbags still lining the doorways.

A huge change was about to take place, life began to move forward quickly. At the beginning of September 2007, I put my flat on the market, for various reasons it hadn't really worked out, I found a better solution in a quiet village just a mile from my mum. After six weeks I accepted an offer which was lucky because the housing market had begun to slow down after about ten years of a rising market, and problems in the economy were making house sales a little harder.

I had an email from Kim (my medical friend who'd helped me so much years before) asking if I'd heard about the book 'The Perrin Technique' and was it worth a look? Despite coming across so many claims over the years of miracle treatments for people with M.E, they were usually unfruitful, something about this made me send for the book immediately. When it arrived, after reading the introduction about an Osteopath who had spent over 18 years doing research on M.E and was having very successful results with a technique he had developed, I couldn't put it down and despite tired eyes and brain exhaustion I finished it in less than two days. I was so excited, it made so much sense and fitted my history of health and injury problems going back to age 14 years. The author knew so much about the illness and even quirky things that I thought were just my symptoms were biologically explained. It was the most extraordinary book on M.E I had ever read; I knew I had to try the treatment.

'The Perrin Technique by Dr Raymond Perrin. Hammersmith Press. Published 2007'

The technique is obviously more complex than I can

explain here, but this is a simple and brief summary. Dr Perrin a Registered Osteopath viewed the disease as a result of disturbance in the drainage of the central nervous system which affected the actions of the sympathetic nervous system. Prior to chronic fatigue, long term stresses on the sympathetic nervous system whether structural, injury, environmental, viral etc caused the system to overload and break down. This caused the symptoms of chronic fatigue. Dr Perrin also had evidence to prove a back flow of lymphatic fluid (this fluid drains poisons out of the body) this meant that instead of poisons draining away properly they were being pumped in reverse and accumulating around the brain and spine adding to the vicious cycle of chronic fatigue. The treatment aimed to improve drainage and in doing so remove poisons. The sympathetic nervous system could then recover and in time return to full health. Unfortunately, it was more usual to feel worse before the patients' health improves. One of the key parts of recovery is the HALF rule. It was very important to only do half what you think you can throughout the process so that the nervous system can recover. Dr Perrin emphasized that it was the difference between helping someone feel better and curing them.

I found this book a truly remarkable insight into the disease I thought I knew so well, it covers all aspects of M.E.

Shortly after finishing the book, I made an appointment to see the nearest therapist trained in this technique. At the time of writing this there weren't many across the country, so I was very fortunate to find one close enough to me.

At my 1st consultation, I was welcomed warmly by Clive, a very experienced Registered Osteopath with whom I had a strong instinctive feeling that he could and would be able to help me. It was quite a long meeting going over my history. I was inevitably tired but very encouraged by what I had learnt about the treatment. I was given a guide that it would take approximately 12 -18 months, based on my current stage of recovery. I should know by the following spring if it was actually going to work for me. I was given exercises to do three times a day to aid lymphatic drainage.

The first stage, I was likely to worsen, the second stage return to where I was prior to treatment and finally the journey to full recovery.

I have summarized the first 12 weekly treatments to show the effects.

Mental deterioration, poor memory, concentration, and reading difficulties. General fatigue and weakness, sleeping a lot.

At the third session I met Dr Perrin, a wonderful man, incredible to meet someone so knowledgeable about M.E, so enthusiastic and determined to help as many patients as possible with the disease. I felt so privileged to have an hour long session with such a specialist. He said, 'Your prognosis is excellent!' What better news could I receive than that!

The main problem became my leg muscles especially my thighs, tight cramp feelings that made walking, standing and driving very difficult and soon temporarily impossible. I also suffered from headaches, sinus pain and intense heat in my back especially my spine. Despite having spent the majority of the previous six weeks needing bed rest almost '24/7' I still had such an extraordinary strong sense of how powerful this treatment was going to be for me. It was the strongest 'gut' feeling I'd had for twenty-two years. Not only did I have such faith in the process, but in my therapist. Clive's encouragement was so supportive, I felt so lucky to have found someone so skilled in his work, understanding, patient and determined to help me become well.

I still felt reasonably well in myself it's just that my legs wouldn't work. I couldn't sit or stand for more than 30 seconds without pain and severe tightness in my thighs and a little in my calves. If I pushed through the aches it just spread further up my leg and took longer to recover. A familiar pattern had returned, I'd experienced it for so many years. When I was able to do menial tasks such as have a shower, I had to sit in the bath, standing was impossible, my legs would have buckled under me. Some of the old fatigue would suddenly swamp my entire system but it didn't linger for too long at a time. I had been warned by Dr Perrin that it would be a really tough time for me, he was right, I had been taken right back to the heart of my illness, I had no choice but to carry on.

It was extraordinary how much of an effect the treatment was having on me, reliving all of my old symptoms, and only under my bodies 'own steam' the most natural way of all, rather than something like homeopathy that helps push symptoms out. I felt much happier working at the healing process in this way. I just had to keep going and come out through the other side.

The first stage, the anticipated deterioration had taken twice as long with me as anticipated to work through, but by the second stage, with Treatment 13, I began to shift from this beginning to feel a little better after each session with Clive.

For the next three months I maintained weekly visits. I began to drive very short distances, just to the village shops at first, eventually reaching a round trip of twelve miles, but was still fatigued after that. A little exercise involved a few minutes walking or on my mum's exercise bike, at a sedate pace and a short distance. My symptoms still returned moderately between good days, making progress extremely arduous and slow, hindered by a long bout of insomnia. I knew I should be sticking to Dr Perrins' 'half rule' but if I did much less I would be spending most of the day needing bed rest with maybe just a little stroll around the garden, that was too frustrating. I wasn't really over exceeding my activities but getting the balance right was hard. I was taking two steps forward and at times still one back but looking at it month by month I was heading in the right direction.

An ongoing, underlying stress was the sale of my flat, six months on from first accepting an offer, paper work connected to the leasehold still had to be sorted out and every day I had the anxiety that my buyers would pull out, especially as daily newspaper headlines and TV bulletins emphasized the worsening of the global economy, mortgage difficulties and the falling prices and sales in the housing market.

CHAPTER TWENTY - SEVEN

My worst fears came true. My buyers pulled out of the sale. For two days my energy ran away from me, it was so important to me to sell my flat and move on, I desperately wanted the new flat I had made an offer on. Incredibly, considering the poor state of the housing market, the next day, I had a viewing, an acceptable offer was made on the spot. The ball was rolling again. It took almost another three months for the sale to complete and by the time moving day arrived my body crashed.

The previous week had been filled with last minute activities that can only be done shortly before a move. In the early hours, two nights before completion on my flat, I began to shake badly, deep fatigue controlled what seemed like every cell in my body. Nausea rolled over me every time I moved, there was no question, I couldn't cope with moving. I was really concerned about my health; it had been many years since I had felt as bad. At 5am I began making out a list of everything that needed doing, where things were and tried to think of someone who could take over for me. I needn't have worried, my kind, thoughtful brother Alistair offered without question to do anything that was necessary. Bearing in mind it was a working day, it wasn't an easy thing for him to take time off. I couldn't have managed without him.

Four weeks later after a severe relapse and recovering at my mums house, I began a new journey in my life, in a nearby village. Treatments with Clive continued. I was sure they were still helping but the stress of such a difficult year moving (in the end it took almost ten months from putting my flat on the market to finally living in my new home) had really taken its toll, I felt I was about six months further behind with his treatments than I should have been.

Talking with Clive one day brought my thoughts back to a treatment I had looked into briefly the previous year, in fact just prior to starting the Perrin Technique. It was called the Lightning Process devised by an osteopath, who incidentally, Clive knew many years previously. I had put it aside as I felt the Perrin Technique was more suitable for me at the time. I re-read the book I had on the Lightning Process and then bought a DVD that had only been available for a few months, this enlightened me further, I began to have more of a conviction that it could make a difference in my recovery.

The Lightning Process by Phil Parker published by Nipton 2007

It was a difficult concept to describe to anyone. It would be easy to think that it was saying that you needed just to think differently, that changing your thoughts could make you better. That implied that it was all in the mind, but the book and the DVD made it clear that it DEFINITLEY wasn't all in the mind, M.E was a genuine and real physical illness, well of course I knew that. (A more detailed explanation will be given later) Clive's encouraging words helped me make that final decision to go ahead with it.

At the end of October 2008, I tentatively called the nearest 'trainer' in the process, Ben. One of the reasons I had delayed enquiring before was that the nearest destination for the seminar was an hour away and that felt like hundreds of miles to me not about thirty-five. The course itself was also approximately four hours each day for three consecutive days. That really worried me. It was far exceeding anything that I had achieved for twenty-two years. I'm a determined woman, and I knew deep down I had to take this chance, I'd done a lot of research and had a very open mind to it.

A lengthy chat with Ben convinced me. I really liked the sound of him, his voice, he showed empathy, with strength behind his conviction of the process. After speaking with him, I knew I had to go ahead with it, if I got there and after an hour I couldn't manage I would come straight home. I had already filled out the application form and sent it straight off. A few days later he called me, after a further chat accepted my suitability for the training course, to be taken within the next month. I understood it was a training, not a treatment. It was up to me, solely me to use the process to help my recovery. No one else could do it for me.

The week before the seminar, I did my best to block it out, it was so daunting for me. My new partner of only a few weeks, Dick, was taking me and would be with me all the time to support me.

Lying on the back seat of Dick's car, my journey had begun. Less than an hour later we were in Cheltenham, the venue had been changed, but this actually suited me better. After booking into the hotel, (I hadn't been in one for about twenty-five years, so this was daunting in itself) I had half an hours rest before making my way, a five minute walk to the seminar. There were two others joining me on the course. Ben welcomed us all warmly and took us into the room to begin the course.

I sat intently listening eagerly to everything being said and watching the projection on the wall. The process intrigued me. During the four hours I did have symptoms, muscle aches, mental fatigue, but somehow my desire to learn kept me going. Towards the later part of the afternoon Ben began to teach us the Lightning Process which in itself began to make a small change very quickly. The easiest way to describe it is from a summary later explained to me by Ben.

'The mind and body are interconnected, they can't be separated. When stress is switched on, you have physical symptoms. The Lightning Process (LP) switches off stress using body and mind'

This is an exceptionally brief explanation and as I later discovered it really does need the three days to learn about it, understanding it fully, but something was already happening.

That evening Dick and I tried to go out for a meal nearby, but I was having trouble getting to grips with LP and had already exceeded my usual limits by managing the four hour seminar exceptionally well, extraordinarily well. Tears trickled down my cold cheeks, winter had come, it was a bitter evening. Returning to the hotel, Dick left again to bring a take away meal back. After a brief rest I then managed to stay up for a couple of hours, and actually felt very well which astonished me. When I finally went to bed, within a few minutes of lying down I felt a wonderful warmth envelope my entire body. It was I thought a 'normal' body temperature, something I hadn't experienced for over twenty-five years. I'd had circulation problems since my teens. I lay smiling, enjoying this phenomenal feeling.

We were given some homework to do and to achieve something 'fun' before the next day's seminar. My idea of fun was to go shopping, I was usually limited to half an hour before fatigue set in. Leaving the hotel with Dick we set out into the November bracing wind. I had to do the LP three or four times during the HOUR I was shopping. It wasn't an easy thing to do in public, so had to do it as best that I could, but it did help. Importantly, I wasn't 'pushing' through the symptoms, as I would have tried to do in previous years, just using everything I had been taught by Ben. Each time I felt symptoms, the LP took me through them, I was able to carry on shopping, until I felt I really needed to lie down briefly. Back at the hotel I only had thirty minutes rest, enough to keep me going. A few tears again, trying to keep the process going and not 'giving' in. I was so pleased at the length of time I'd been out, and here I was again off to do another four hours at the seminar. The LP was taught to us in more detail and again progress was made during that time. Straight after the course, I had a quick shower at the hotel and then as my second 'fun' thing to do, Dick and I decided to go out for a meal as we hadn't managed it the previous night.

Walking to a restaurant I felt incredibly well. I hadn't been out to dinner for at least eight years, nothing was phasing me. No symptoms, no worries, I felt so relaxed, my face alight with joy. I had a wonderful meal, especially a rich chocolate mud pudding with no after effects from having rich food. It was probably the most memorable meal I'd ever had. Walking back to the hotel on a drizzly damp evening I continued to stay up until 9.15pm when I felt 'normally' tired, not 'M.E' tired. I was totally astounded at my achievements that day. I had real evidence that LP could and WAS working for me.

Out shopping on the third morning after doing some homework for Ben, it was still a struggle at times to maintain the process and let it help me. I deliberately avoided looking at my watch to see how long I'd been out, but we were short of time and had to check out of the hotel by midday. Anxiety set in, tears filled my eyes. Lack of time meant that I only had 10 minutes to have a rest before leaving the hotel room and then we had to sit at reception for about forty minutes until leaving to walk to the final days seminar. Dick reassured me and helped me through this little 'blip'. By 12.45pm we were on our way, I had recovered and was ready to learn the final stages of this remarkable training.

At the end of the course, it seemed so strange to be going home. This was really the start of my new life. Something remarkable had definitely taken place during the three days. After a brief shop in the centre of Cheltenham again, and a cup of tea at the hotel reception where we had to return to collect our luggage, we set off for the hours' drive home. This time I was sitting in the front seat. Through the dark, foggy night the oncoming car lights had no effect on me at all. In previous years I would have been exhausted after about 20 minutes watching the brightness heading towards me. Once home and after a twenty minute much needed rest, I was up for another couple of hours before bed. Totally bewildered at all the outstanding achievements I had made in such a short space of time.

The following morning, I went to see my mum, she beamed and hugged me,

"Are you a new person? "

"I think so! " I said doing my best to hold back some tears.

I recounted as best as I could my adventures but had to do LP several times to keep going, it was working, I had to be consistent with it. Returning home to my flat, the best was yet to come. By 10pm I realised I had been up ALL day! This was the most remarkable thing. I had been unable to do this for twenty-two years! Not even coming close, the least amount of rest I had needed during all these years was 5 hours a day. I curled up into my cosy bed, the white sheets were cold, my thick duvet snuggled up over my shoulders, my mind in a contented daze.

The next three to four days were a particular challenge, I needed to do the process about ten times a day, but it continued to prove effective. I was getting continuous evidence that it worked. By the second week I was walking thirty minutes three times, I hadn't done that for about 16 years! I loved the freedom. I drove the route I had walked, measuring the distance. In total 1.8 miles! Unbelievable, I keep using that word, but it was. My legs were aching from being unused, not M.E legs.

Ben told me that usually the process becomes

automatic, needing to use LP less and less, anything from one day to about a month, as long as it was practised consistently when needed. One day, tears flowed. It's difficult for me to understand, let alone recount to others what was going through my mind at this time. Finally, really believing that I was truly becoming well, letting go of so many destroyed years of my life. I couldn't let myself dwell on that, I had to let go and see my way ahead to a new life, a healthy life.

To anyone with M.E reading this chapter they may well think it's impossible to have been desperately ill for so many years and to suddenly be making so much progress at the rate I was, it really didn't make sense. I, more than anyone who has been through so much would be the first to feel that way and be extremely sceptical about the process. I had been genuinely very, very unwell for many, many years. It was actually very hard for me to accept, that with everything I have been through it only took 3 days to convince me that I could finally alter my life.

It took a year of thorough research to decide that it was the right process for me, I believe that's not unusual, LP hadn't actually been around for that long, or I should say not being used as successfully for patients with M.E for long. With many so called therapies available, it's hard to know sometimes just what to go ahead and try, as still no one therapy helps everyone. Too many treatments I'd tried had the opposite effect, making me extremely unwell, taking me to a point of not wanting to continue with my life. There came a point when I had to be so careful to say yes to 'anything'. I've personally hated it when people have said to me, 'You must try such and such a treatment, my friend has got better, it must help you.' That's not the case. M.E is a complex disease and different therapies work differently for all. When you have tried many things for many years, no matter how desperately you want to get better, it's actually tiring and often more demoralising to keep trying more, unless you are really ready for it, and really believe it could work. For LP in particular, I needed to be open minded. It would be very easy for anyone to dismiss LP training as agreeing with so many disbelievers that M.E was 'all in the mind', it is absolutely, categorically NOT.

My knowledge of the background is too limited and may put off many as thinking they have tried something similar and it didn't work for them, therefore this training wouldn't. This was a very unique and powerful process. In simplistic terms, the three day course involved learning how to manage the bodies acute stress response.

I still find it very hard to believe how effective it had been for me. I'm so lucky and grateful to have had Dick join me during the seminar, he was always there to support me and fully understood what I was doing, it made such a difference to my recovering strength and energy.

For many years I had always thought that all I needed was a 'switch flicked' somewhere in me, to turn on my energy that had been malfunctioning for so long, then I would be well again. This 'switch' it seemed, had now been flicked! It looked as though I'd finally found my breakthrough; it was working for me.

NOTE: To my knowledge, it appeared that LP was very helpful for many, including myself, but not the complete answer for everyone.
Skipping forward momentarily to the year 2021: The underlying theory behind LP, aiming to calm the 'flight or fight' stress response, in my understanding, had elements in its basis used by the NHS to help treat patients suffering with fatigue from Long Covid.

CHAPTER TWENTY - EIGHT

My life continued to surprise me, doing things I'd been unable to do for so long. My first trip to the seaside for twenty-three years holds a great memory for me. Dick took me to Bournemouth for two days, a place I had never been to. (It's the nearest sandy beach to me, a two and a half hour drive) For Spring it was amazingly warm sunshine with at times perfect clear blue skies. I spent most of the time saying, 'I'm at the sea! There's the sea!' Feeling the sand beneath my toes relived a long-lost feeling, scrunching my digits tightly and then letting the fine, dry beige flecked particles filter through the gaps. The April sea temperature was like ice! I had to step in though, too much time had passed since I'd paddled like this, I had to experience it again, but it was too cold to stay and jump over rippling creeping waves.

On the second day I marveled at the way the mist can come in so quickly from the sea, one minute the pier was visible, the next smothered in a dense film. I'd forgotten this simple feature of nature. I'm so used to seeing it inland, but there's something mystifying watching it over the ocean.

I was tired after my little holiday, but I recovered quickly. I was still building my physical stamina, so that new large challenges did still tire me, but on a very different scale than previously.

By August 2009 I had achieved eleven out of fifteen goals that I had set myself many years ago, for example, going to the seaside, walking for an hour, being up all day, going to the cinema, and playing tennis.

Being able to play tennis was such a thrill for me. For a long time I had often wondered if I would ever play again due my neck/shoulder injury aged fourteen. Dick used to coach tennis and was very impressed with my first session after almost twenty-five years. I was too! I had seriously questioned myself as to whether I would get the ball over the net having been away from the game so long. Dick lent me a racket, it felt peculiar but exciting to hold, I tested the grip several times. On this beautiful early summers evening, the court was bathed in sunlight, I was so exhilarated and played with great confidence despite clearly needing to re-learn to judge the timing of the ball! My lack of stamina meant I often had to let the ball bounce twice before hitting it. After fifteen minutes I was 'puffed' out, but without doubt, tired from purely being unfit not 'M.E' tired, a DEFINITE difference, a fantastic feeling! I couldn't believe I was at last playing my favourite sport again and LOVING it. Dick said it was clear I had a talent for the game.

That was the start of almost weekly lessons, each time improving significantly and so important for me in many ways. I was really gently flowing into a 'normal' life. Of everything I was doing it was playing tennis where it became most noticeable to see improvement in my overall fitness.

I was using the Lightning Process when needed, it was still pushing me forward, although admittedly I probably should have used it more at times to move me further on more quickly.

I knew I still needed to work on my stamina and confidence to fully accept that I was so much better, but it got easier all the time. I was sure all I needed to do was to continue to build on my physical fitness; my key to everything fluently rolling along in my life.

CHAPTER TWENTY - NINE

In February 2010 I had to deal with the worst thing that could possibly happen to me: my mum passed away suddenly, unable to survive emergency surgery after three weeks in hospital prior to this. I was utterly distraught, devastated. My old symptoms flooded my system once more, an unexpected release of such immense emotional stress.

Out of 44 years, I had lived with her for 41, unusual for someone of my age, but because of M.E that's the direction life had taken us. We were so close and understood each other so well. She was the only person who totally understood my life, having given everything of herself to care for me for many, many years, worrying herself literally sick about me in the process. Shadowing every step of my debility and recovery, guiding, endlessly supportive, and completely devoted. My only true ally had gone.

I will never forget how deeply distressed she was after being treated appallingly on a home visit by a Psychiatrist. After a lengthy chat with me the Psychiatrist spoke to my mum, accused her bluntly of having 'Munchausen by proxy syndrome', a mental illness where a care giver falsely creates or exaggerates an illness of a person in their care typically a / their child, essentially accusing my mum of making me ill. It is considered a form of child abuse. This instantly shook my mum so badly that in a very rare outburst from her usual quiet nature, in equally blunt words she shouted at the clinician, *"How dare you accuse me of that, get out of my house"*. Thankfully this wasn't followed up by social services. I'm assuming the Psychiatrist must have changed her opinion on my case. During the first ten years in particular, this was the kind of negative, total misunderstanding we were still getting from some clinicians, thankfully not all of them. I'm just so sad that my mum had to be put through this disbelief as well as myself.

I switched between days of numbness with grief to those of being overwhelmed with tears and finding it unbearable. Words can't express the enormity of how much my mum meant to me, and how much I miss her to this day and will forever. It was and still is such a desperate, isolating feeling to want to see, or at least hear someone's voice more than anything you could ever want, with some realisation that you never will. I am comforted by the fact that I have her genes in me and part of her survives within me all the time, forever. I must remember that. I am lucky enough to inherit her tender, gentle, loving, giving nature and her hazel coloured eyes.

I felt so alone and as though I no longer belonged to anyone. My connection was broken. I found it much harder, not having children, I couldn't throw myself into a new life with no mother by being a mother myself: I should have been by that time in my life. I had no one to pass on my soul, my physical inheritance. No one to teach everything I knew, to pass on through generations. No one to pass on such love that I had to give. I don't think the majority of people would truly understand that unless they were in the same position.

Both my parents were wonderful, wonderful people, loved by many. I will treasure everything they ever taught me. I love and miss them both terribly.

During August 2010 I was given the opportunity by an old family friend to work a few hours a week in a local Estate Agents office. It was a timely offer as I needed the money to help me keep going. I started with two afternoons a week, four hours at a time. It was mentally very tiring at the start. I loved saying to anyone and everyone; "I have a job, I'm off to work this afternoon!" I had such a buzz from knowing I was actually working after so many years. Working at the Vets ten years previously was on a different scale, my health poles apart from then.

I did find doing a few extra hours very hard at first, covering for illness or holiday, I was most comfortable doing 8 - 12 hours a week to give me time and energy to keep on top of the rest of my life. During the next year I became more confident at work, my duties including secretarial, administration, viewings and using my easy going, non-pushy nature to try and sell properties.

I still forgot to use the Lightning process as often as I should, I became comfortable being able to do so much more than I had for decades, that I unconsciously became a little stuck in a rut at times.

I moved home, putting my flat up To Let. I looked after the management myself becoming a Landlord for the first time. It consumed quite a bit of time, most importantly giving me extra income.

I had two goals yet to achieve, a trip abroad; timing and money had something to do with the delay in that, as well as a huge dose of faith in my health; now a millions times better, if not perfect. The second was my lifelong dream, desire and need to bring about the reality of why I felt I was put onto this earth; to become a mother. Still grieving daily for my own mother, I genuinely couldn't see a point in my life continuing long term without this huge hole of grief I had felt for years of being childless being filled. My GP thankfully agreed that my health was now not a problem where that was concerned, It wasn't impossible for me to still be a mother, but it was probably going to mean going down the donor / IVF route. Time would tell.

EPILOGUE TWO

If someone tells you they have cancer, (although thankfully many cancers are treatable nowadays) it will have on most people an instant impact knowing that person has a serious disease. I hope that one day when anyone mentions M.E most people will immediately understand the severity of illness this name brings, it will have the same impact on people as with more well-known disabling diseases.

For me the following summarises thoughts I wish I'd portrayed to many people over the years to try and make them understand what it was like for me. It may sound extreme, but it was my reality, and the trouble is, as my mum often said, it's just too terrible for people to want to think about.

Imagine you are twenty-one years old, go home to your parents' house now, close the door behind you, go up to your bedroom, lie down and stay there for approximately 18-24 hours a day. For lengthy periods you are in constant pain, unbearable pain, feeling desperately unwell. At the worst times the only way to communicate is by eye movements because you have so little energy, your body can barely function, it has almost completely shut down. You frequently lose the ability to speak because the muscles that make your vocal cords function are so weak as the rest of your body, that you can't talk for weeks at a time. In the rare hours you are able to be out of bed, you might only be able to crawl to the bathroom, lie on the floor for 20 minutes until you have the stamina to crawl back to bed. You can never go more than 10 miles from your house, you can never have a week's holiday, you can't have visitors for more than an hour maximum, you lose friends, your independence, and your reason for living. This is not just for a few days, a few weeks, not six months, but twenty-two years. Remember this is not out of choice. Not because, for some bizarre reason as I had people suggest to me in the earlier years, that I was lazy, couldn't be bothered with life so it was easier for me to stay in bed all the time! That is the kind of attitude I was dealing with at times.

To anyone who doesn't understand M.E, can you imagine that? No, it's just too terrible and unbearable to think of. Well, that's been my life.

Finally, to anyone with M.E that has found the energy to read my book, please do not be discouraged by the length of time I've been unwell. Beliefs and attitudes by the medical profession have now changed, although it's taken a long time. Treatments have progressed and scientists now study the illness at a level unheard of when I was first diagnosed. As you will know all too well, everyone with M.E is affected in different ways and manages the illness in different ways.

Mine has been an incredibly long battle and a journey through life I'd of course, rather not have taken. A combination of therapies, in particular Chris's treatments from Australia, The Perrin Technique and the final missing link to strengthen things further, The Lightning Process have all been necessary to my recovery path.

It may not always have seemed like it but each day that passed was a day nearer to a better life, a healthier life I longed for and deserved.

PART THREE

CHAPTER THIRTY

Life was generally moving forward; I was full of hope and enthusiasm. Work at the estate agents continued to give me some drive in life, I still needed to plan how my day was structured to allow me to have the energy to work for a three or four hour shift and remain focused whilst there. My days off were relatively quiet but even so required a considerable amount of rest.

How oblivious I was, as my prolonged battle was far from over.

One of the biggest struggles I had mentally was that apart from a couple of two-day trips to the English coast with Dick, they were the only times I'd been able to leave my local surroundings except for being in hospital, I hadn't had a true holiday for 26 years. Some readers might be able to appreciate how they feel if they've missed three or four years when they haven't been able to go on holiday for whatever reason. Imagine making that 26 years when there hasn't even been a single weekend away, it's very hard going on the mind and soul.

I frequently ran over in my mind everything that I was now able to achieve. My biggest goal had always been a holiday abroad but there were many years when I doubted I would ever achieve this again.

Knowing I had the full support of my partner Dick, who understood me and my limitations as much as anybody could, I made an enormous decision. Within days of this I had booked a holiday to Corsica, it was one of the nearest countries that seemed most suitable for my needs and requirements. I was a nervous wreck leading up to the departure, but I had planned everything to the nearest minute that I could, clearly needing to allow for any delays along the way. Mentally I broke down the journey into many sections, we stayed the night before at an airport hotel to break up the journey, it was only a two hour flight to the glorious warm sunshine. Sitting on a plane was the most bizarre thing, I felt like a teenager buzzing with excitement but at the same time that thrill was also draining. There was no turning back now.

Dick was incredible I couldn't have done this without him, he knew me so well. On arrival at the tiny self-catering accommodation, I collapsed on the bed unable to move, I had totally burnt myself out which wasn't at all surprising. I stayed there until the next day. Dick went to find some food as I just couldn't leave the bed. We were only 5 minutes from the beach but an incredibly steep decline to it, we had hired a car so over the next few days I managed some sunbathing, in awe of the view that was before my eyes and realisation of what I had achieved, where I was. I'd never seen such a beautiful location. It truly felt like a dream. I did have some small panic attacks needing to rest throughout the day and only really managed because I was lying on the beach much of the time, doing very little walking, but did manage some short trips in the car to see some of the island.

Almost no English was spoken in the area where we were, so finding a little memory of O'Level French helped tick things along! The warmth of the sunshine and the change in climate did me the world of good.

I was so sad to leave because I couldn't imagine when I'd manage a holiday abroad again, this had been so immensely special and important to me. We'd had such a wonderful time together despite my limitations.

Luck wasn't on my side though, returning to Stansted Airport I couldn't believe that my luggage had been lost, especially as the case couldn't have stood out much more, a pale grey with huge white spots! The stress levels drained me of what little energy I had.

We returned home whereupon I just crashed, feeling extremely nauseous with fatigue, my legs had given up on me.

My luggage was never found, apparently these days there are only a very tiny proportion of cases that are never found. I had to try and see the funny side of it in one way; the allowance had been 23 kgs, because I hadn't been on holiday for so many years, I had no idea what to take, so I'd 'maxed out' my weight allowance with virtually my whole summer wardrobe! At least my insurance replaced many things, but I had taken a few items of my mums clothing that I loved, so I was a little emotional to know I would never see them again.

This trip abroad was an incredible milestone for me, I was so proud of myself needing to keep looking at photographs to prove to myself I had been there.

The other most important area of my life I desperately wanted to change was to fulfil the enormous hole I had to become a mother. I had finally reached a point in my recovery where upon I felt I was well enough to be able to look after a child. To watch them grow, develop, thrive, and engulf them with so much love that I still had inside me aching to envelop my own family. I and my partner saw a specialist on the NHS but was totally distraught to find I was only just too old for this. I was under the impression I still had a little time left. It didn't help that at that time there were several high-profile female celebrities that were having children well into their 40s. It wasn't until a few years later that it became more widely publicised that several of these births were purely by egg donation, a rather important fact that was well hidden at the time. I can't have been the only one who gained hope from seeing these more mature women having children at that age. It actually felt as though I had been cruelly deceived by these women, but I couldn't blame them for taking the actions they needed to, hiding their personal circumstances. Of course, everyone is entitled to their privacy. I more than most people could understood their immense desire to be a mother by whatever means necessary.

My only option was to go to a private London clinic and have egg donation. The huge expense this entailed and appreciation that the child would have no part of me genetically was personally something I couldn't pursue.

CHAPTER THIRTY - ONE

I'm going to go into detail here regarding childlessness, a subject that is rarely talked about, it's so important in my life, that to me it should be noted of something of great value in my story.

The emotional pain rips through my heart, through my soul, every day. Sometimes distraction is all I need to relieve the ache, other days the moment I see children or babies on TV I immediately have to turn over the channel. I just can't bear it.

I knew from my early teens that my main goal in life was to become a mother, there was an intensity in my soul, it was a natural path for me, for many women. At that age you don't assume that life will veer very far from the norm. Finish school maybe go to college, university, get a job, find a partner / husband, start a family. I was meant to be that person, just an ordinary life, not particularly ambitious, a wife and mother, potentially a grandmother too. That would have more than satisfied my inner being with other goals, achievements, adventures, and fun surrounding this core of motherhood.

I was a very happy child, very fortunate to grow up with a very content happy loving family, my parents and three siblings all got along so well and cared deeply for each other. I dreamed of emulating this scenario just as many people would, do. But, as you now know aged 21 contracting Glandular Fever, my life from that point would change forever particularly regarding motherhood.

When my dad passed away suddenly, I was just 27 years old, as the youngest of four children, the only one remaining at home full time, because I was still so unwell. I had to try and care for my mum (alongside the help of my sibling's when they visited) who struggled with intense grief. This period of time, looking after my mum revived my intense desire to be a mum, but I was still desperately unwell. My clock was ticking, although I had a few years left in me there was still a chance.

As I saw it, there were six main groups with subcategories, I may not have covered every possibility:

1. Those who want children, find it easy, go ahead having a family.
2. Those who didn't plan a family, but it happens anyway.
3. Those who never wanted children anyway.
4. Those who have difficulty conceiving but are successful with IVF, or those who have at least tried IVF, become pregnant who miscarry.
5. Those who maybe lost a child through miscarriages or possibly passed away at a young age who decided to adopt or foster.
6. A tiny minority in the world who like me who have always been desperate to be a mother, whose every cell in their being has a deep womanly natural need to be a mother but have never been pregnant. For various reasons

have not been able to or wanted to adopt or foster.

The outcome of a deeply seated need in my core to be a mother, to be called 'mummy', will unbearably never happen.

I believe many people never give any real thought to their fortune to be a parent, it just happens. They go through ups and downs, difficulties, highs and lows through the process of being a parent. Of course, it's incredibly hard work and exhausting, to mention just a couple of words and phrases that summarise parental care.

I'm certain a good many never really think how mind-blowing the creation is they have made, to really and truly acknowledge they have been so fortunate and lucky to create another human being, to really reflect what that means. To create a new life, carrying your genetics, creating a part of you into a new being. To teach, to love, to help create a whole new life. As they grow seeing elements of their own personality and physical features, good or bad. To be able to watch their part creation grow and learn.

Without realising it I think many enjoy the chance to go back over their own childhood memories the games they played, a chance to relive their youth, of which may have been carefree or the opposite where you are determined your child has a better life than you did. This is a generalisation of course not all parents are able to financially, practically, or even emotionally give in the same way that I would have hoped, aimed to do. Maybe many don't really have much interest in their child.

I have an abundance of love that's been burning in me for more than three decades, I've never been able to transfer that to a growing child so longed for.

These are not idyllic thoughts, I'm very aware of all the complications, worries and strains in every area of life including other relationships a growing child can make. They are just pure rational, reasonable thoughts of a woman whose natural maternal desire has always been so strong and has never come to fruition.

My daily challenge continues, there is nothing anyone can ever say that will ease the pain I feel. All I can do is try and block it out, distract myself which becomes harder again with a new cycle, generation of my friends and family on their way to one day becoming grandparents. How many of them do you hear doting on their new generation, how wonderful to be a grandparent to see your child starting a new cycle of life. I will never be a granny, the hurt will continue for the rest of my life, it's too deep a human desire for me to ever let go of.

CHAPTER THIRTY - TWO

Early 2013 brought immense sadness to me, Dick and I split up. I can't underestimate to the reader enough how important he, the relationship was to me. I didn't think any partner could truly understand and accept me for the immense limitations I had. If it hadn't been for him, I genuinely wouldn't have been where I was with my progress. When my mum died, if he hadn't supported my shattered being, broken inside and out, given me such emotional strength, I truly believe I wouldn't have continued with my life. I don't say that lightly.

We did however remain as friends, just a few months later he agreed to accompany me on a holiday to Malta. He completely understood how much the previous year's trip to Corsica had meant to me and how much of an achievement that was, I felt so strongly I needed to prove to myself I could manage another trip abroad, importantly with someone who knew exactly how to care for me when things got too much.

Despite our recent split, we had a wonderful trip with lots of laughter. One of the biggest highlights in my life to this day was to swim with dolphins. I can completely understand people's abhorrence of dolphins in captivity, it might seem to the contrary but I'm with them on that, but when you're there and understand how they are cared for, it's very clear to see the love the trainers have for them and the enjoyment the dolphins find playing with humans is truly quite magical.

Since watching Torvill and Dean win the Olympics in 1984 I'd had a strong desire to skate. In my teens my mum and dad had taken me to Oxford to an area on the Plains that used to frequently flood and freeze in the winter, it was a popular place for people to come, have fun and skate. I used my mums' old skates; they were very old! I could stand up and skate a little in my own style rather than any precise technique. Oxford had a good skating rink, I'd never had the opportunity to go there before, longing to find a new hobby I joined up for the autumn term beginner's class.

In my youth I was a competent all-round sports achiever, every new sport I tried I did well at, excelled in many, it seemed skating was no different. I absolutely loved it! There were about a dozen in my group. I picked up the moves easily and soon found myself teaching a couple of the others who were lagging behind whilst the coach focused on those having the most difficulty. I did find it very tiring, but it was such a thrill, it reminded me of the same sensation when skiing downhill in my teens. The cool air whistling by my face, the freedom of speed.

Early in the second term I was doing so well that the coach asked me if I wanted to move up to the advanced class, I jumped at the chance. That word 'jumped' was about to become my downfall, literally! Five minutes into my lesson practising how to jump I caught the toe pick incorrectly, with all my body weight landing on my left bent wrist! Not long after I found myself at the minor injuries' unit as an emergency on gas and air for the pain. My wrist was pulled back into place, I had two fractures. For the next few weeks, I made several trips to the John Radcliffe in Oxford, three plaster casts later, lots of physio it took five months to heal.

The week after my last physio session ended I was heading for another lengthy spell of injury.

A beautiful spring day enticed me outside to begin sanding down my patio doors in need of a refreshing coat of paint. I was about to get a step ladder but decided that I could make a start using an old wooden chair to stand on. We'd had an extremely damp winter; I hadn't realised the chair had become rotten. Within seconds of standing on one leg about to bring the other leg onto it, my foot went through straight onto the paving stone beneath with such force that it split my heel in two and shattered my ankle bone. Within an hour I was being driven in an ambulance with sirens, blue lights flashing up to the John Radcliffe for emergency surgery. It seems if I hadn't had surgery so quickly there were serious concerns that I may have never been able to walk normally again.

After five days in hospital, I was sent home. I'd

never had a general anaesthetic before, I couldn't believe that because of my history of fatigue it took a month for this to wear off completely. I was absolutely exhausted from the ordeal. Living on my own I had an incredibly difficult time. I wasn't in a plaster cast as I now had two very large titanium screws holding my foot together, so I had to be non-weight bearing on my right leg for the first six weeks, which basically meant resting with my leg up all day.

I think I must have watched every episode of Midsomer Murders! With my left wrist only just healed from that fracture it was hard manoeuvring around the house and looking after myself, but my neighbours were great, I was so lucky to have them. Between them and my friends they did everything they could to try and help. I needed a further 8 weeks in a boot then six weeks on crutches, a total of five months off work.

Time ticked on. I had my routines allowing me to feel reasonably stable, if still leading a limited lifestyle. This continued for the next three years until in 2016, I had no other choice than to walk away from my job.

It was a very difficult time for me, an unnecessary amount of stress put upon me that caused my health to suffer immensely. I'd given so much of myself to that job, frequently pushing myself beyond my energy means, smiling and carrying on, suffering at home later. I strongly disagreed with some of the work ethics, feeling I couldn't be a part of that environment anymore. I won't elaborate further.

There was one glimmer of hope to help me move forward a little. Whilst working at the agents I had become friends with the inventory clerk that we used for rental properties, I asked him directly if he had any work available.

With a short period of rest to begin to pull myself together I soon began work as an inventory clerk. It was very part time, only a few hours a week but that's all I could cope with, I was rather thrown in at the deep end and took a while to settle in. The work suited me because I'm very methodical, practical, and observant.

My role involved one of three things. Either arriving at a rental property to meet the new tenants, running over the inventory with them and explaining some general regulations that needed to be adhered to. Or, at the end of a tenancy I would meet the tenants and study the property carefully looking for any irregularities against the original inventory, for example damage or anything that was beyond fair wear and tear. I'd then write up a report that went back to the agent or landlord for them to decide whether the tenants would have their full deposit returned to them. In an extreme case my report would be used to help settle any disputes in court. You can possibly imagine how awful some of the properties were that I saw, on the other hand I was privileged to see some of the most beautiful properties. I thoroughly enjoyed most of the properties I saw but I did find the driving very tiring and was restricted in the distance I could travel.

The third part of the job was carrying out the inventory itself. I hated this role; I'd look at something like a front door lock and have a mental block as to which type of lock it was! It took me far too long to dictate my inventories, they were incredibly detailed and with the many hundreds of photos that had to go with it. Eventually it was agreed I would just check in and checkout tenants, it was far less tiring for me in general.

CHAPTER THIRTY - THREE

'Twenty-twenty' rolled off the tongue so easily, it somehow seemed like the year ahead would be a joyful one, but not so, that couldn't have been further from the reality.

Early into the new decade news reports from China were talking about a deadly virus spreading to Europe. Recalling TV scenes in Italy, hospitals flooded with seriously ill patients, many were dying, the staff wearing highly protective outfits, it looked like something out of a Hollywood movie. Indications were that it would soon spread to this country. I watched the news and genuinely couldn't quite believe such events could ever appear in this country. About three weeks later I listened in disbelief to the Prime Minister who asked us, *ordered* us all to stay at home. As we now know this was the start of one of the most horrific times in our country's history. The deadly virus named Covid-19 was spreading.

During the first week we were ordered to stay at home I had to go to work, I was one of the few professions that were allowed to leave home and still go to work. It was one of the most peculiar experiences. There was barely a car on the road, in parts of the country police were stopping drivers to make sure they were allowed to be out, it made me nervous and uncomfortable.

With this country still in the early days of the

pandemic it took a while to learn new behaviour and adhere to the laws of what became known as 'lockdown'.

I was petrified of getting Covid with my underlying chronic fatigue still lingering in the background. I couldn't begin to imagine how ill I might be if I caught it if I was lucky to survive the infection as so many tens of thousands weren't.

We all had very different and difficult experiences of living with Covid, some far more horrific than others. Those whose loved ones passed away, especially those in hospital or nursing homes where upon restrictions had meant they were unable to be with them in their last days and hours, an unbearable situation.

Into the second year I was starting to struggle. I lost my job as an inventory clerk, my colleagues decided to retire sooner than they had planned, like many people Covid had changed their values on life. I was already finding life hard and difficult to deal with for various reasons so losing my job didn't help matters but I understood their intentions to move their life in a different direction. Such a kind, caring and thoughtful couple I'd been so fortunate to have worked with them.

Being isolated with lockdowns and limitations in seeing friends and family was hard for us all. I started to feel incredibly claustrophobic and slightly anxious, panicky. Being shut in for long periods during the past year had brought back reminders of the many years I had been trapped in my house in the early years of M.E. It was starting to have quite a negative impact on me, I was aware that it wouldn't take too much more to pull me right down.

Travelling locally or especially abroad during the pandemic had been either forbidden or extremely limited to anyone who fitted a certain very constrained criterion. The world was now beginning to open little by little with great caution still required. My fear of sinking deeply mentally led me to make a huge decision.

Since my holiday to Malta, I had travelled three times over three years with one of my best friends Sally to the small island of Menorca. Immense research went into the trip to find a country and location with the most ease of travel for me, putting the least amount of strain, or pressure regarding fatigue. I took the huge plunge and booked a holiday to the same familiar location, this time just for myself. For various reasons no one else was able to come with me at that time. It was probably absolute madness, not only was I going to attempt to travel abroad on my own for the first time since I'd become unwell with M.E but we were still in the middle of a pandemic. An overwhelming not desire, but *need* to escape filled me with positivity.

Travel arrangements were broken up in my mind to cope with each part, to not think too far ahead. I'm a very organised individual who had planned everything with the finest detail especially as extra measures were needed prior to and during the trip to comply with Covid regulations both here and abroad. Trying to mentally allow for any disruptions that might occur with my travel arrangements or my stay, I set off.

All was going quite smoothly until I arrived at the reception to the apartments. I noticed on the desk a large sign saying please book your Covid pre-flight home tests here. Before departing the UK, I'd researched where I had to go to get my Covid antigen test to make sure it was somewhere feasible for me to manage. I should have been able to get the test either at the reception at the hotel or in a small clinic 10 minutes' walk away next to some shops that I knew and had been too many times before, so that would have been fine. I logged on to the website but to my utter dismay found that most of it was in German! Slightly panicked I managed to fill in the request for a test but was shocked to find that there were only three appointments on the day I needed it to be carried out as there were so many tourists wanting to get the pre-flight tests. My two options of the hotel or the nearby clinic were no longer functioning, the only option possible was to go back to the capital city Mahon. I started to really panic. I had no idea how I was going to get there or manage to do that. I knew I had no choice other than to book the appointment because if I didn't, I had no idea how I was going to be tested and therefore be allowed back on the plane home to the UK. I double checked with reception to confirm these arrangements were correct. I was informed that the previous week some tourists had to fly to Majorca with more testing facilities and then return to Menorca because there were no available appointments on the island at that time.

My energy was draining rapidly with the shock of how on earth I was going to deal with all of this. I got the key to my apartment, had a very quick cup of tea, with some chocolate left over from the plane journey. My body and mind completely exhausted but so thrilled to be back. Feeling the intense warmth of the sunshine on my skin, looking out to the turquoise sea I quickly changed and went down to the beach. Almost 100 stone steps down to the boardwalk. The warm sea breeze blowing my sarong in its gentle hold around me. The beach was fairly empty. The majority there were usually Italians, and Spanish. I found a nice spot near the back by some sand dunes, lay down and tried to relax. It became suddenly very apparent that I really wasn't feeling very good, I didn't feel like moving but knew I had to be back in my room resting properly. I gathered my things together and started to walk back along the beach to the steps with a rather dizzy sensation. I seemed to be drifting my way up. Nearing the top, I stumbled, flopped onto a step, I knew I was about to faint. Seconds later I collapsed in a heap unconscious, How I managed this without cracking my head open on the stone step I don't know.

I came around slowly with water being thrown on my head and neck and seven people surrounding me. "Estas Bien? Are you OK?" I heard several times, I heard somebody say in English," The colour is coming back to her face". Another one stating, "Maybe we should cancel the ambulance"? A rather gorgeous Spanish lifeguard offered to go and buy me some Cola from the bar," Si, gracias!" I said quietly. About 15 minutes later most of the people dispersed, the dark-haired lifeguard took hold of my arm and helped me walk the short distance to my apartment along with a lovely young Spanish couple who spoke excellent English. The receptionist from the hotel had been on the scene, she'd said she'd called an ambulance and the police (why the police I don't know?!) because I was unconscious for so long. They were cancelled when I came to. The receptionist very kindly came back to visit me on two occasions before the end of her shift resulting in calling the local doctor to make sure that I was OK. I felt so unwell with the trauma, stress, the heat, and being in a foreign country. It suddenly began to dawn on me where I was and all alone.

I don't really enjoy much about technology but just before I'd left England, I downloaded WhatsApp so that I could at least keep in touch with my sister in New Zealand, and also so that she wouldn't worry to death about me on my own. We spoke virtually every day; she kept encouraging me to keep going. What an incredible achievement it was for me to be there, somehow coping in another country after everything I've been through. She knew more than most just how much effort physically and mentally it had taken for me to be there. She was very proud of me.

I spent the next day and a half in the apartment. I was afraid to go out. It was self-catering, thankfully on my way to it after checking in, I'd stopped at the little supermarket on site and got a few groceries and some water.

On the 3rd and 4th day feeling a little more rested I slowly ventured down to the beach for a few hours each day. The glorious clear, shallow turquoise sea was so inviting, I paddled a little but didn't dare swim. It was about a 50 to 75 metre walk into the sea before it was deep enough to swim, I was still feeling quite weary and was concerned that I might faint again, not the best idea in the sea!

I started to enjoy my holiday. My fingers clenching and letting go of the golden sand that had tiny little red flecks amongst it, closing my eyes listening to the few seagulls swooping down for the odd scrap left by holiday makers.

I had booked a taxi to take me to Mahon for my pre-flight Covid test. I'd asserted my need that the taxi driver must wait for me. On arrival the taxi driver left insisting he couldn't wait, so much for ensuring that he would! I was impressed by the efficiency of the hospital; my test was done quickly with the result due in 15 to 30 minutes via email. After a stressful discussion with a receptionist, she helped me arrange a taxi, I was soon on my way back to the resort.

The next few hours were spent frantically trying to get my result. It seemed I had made an error with my post code on the original booking form using lower case instead of upper for one letter, this caused no end of problems! I was back and forth with the hotel receptionist, I had to ring the hospital with the suggestion I might need to go back at 6:00 p.m. that day and have a new test done which filled me with absolute horror because I knew I had no energy to do that. Finally, I received the result, I can't tell you the relief! I would now be allowed back on the plane and into my home country. To finish off the day I had to fill in a very long Passenger Locator Form which also allowed me to enter the UK, the GOV.UK website was so busy it crashed. I was time limited as to when I could fill this in prior to my departure so stress levels rose higher again. By 7:00 p.m. that evening my return journey was finally arranged with all the necessary online documentation in place. I was so tired my eyes filled with tears, I sat on my bed and like a little girl wanting her mum, then curled in a ball and cried, I just so wished I was at home, I couldn't take anymore. I only had one day left so did my utmost to enjoy the last few hours in one of the most stunning locations in my mind, on earth.

My journey home had a few hiccups, by the time I opened my front door I grabbed a cup of tea and went straight to bed. A couple of weeks later feeling renewed after some considerable rest from my troublesome travels.

To this day, I still don't know how on earth I managed that trip alone, but I'm so proud of myself that I did.

Katie MacLarnon

CHAPTER THIRTY - FOUR

The next few months were spent organising and carrying out quite extensive refurbishment on the apartment that I Let, being hands on as much as I could be, something that I enjoyed.

My role as a Landlord took precedence finding new tenants to rent the property for a few months until early the following spring. I then put the flat on the market, my plan to find a better investment.

Fortunately, all my hard work paid off, the property market was buoyant, my flat sold within a few days. Due to the pandemic some people were deciding on a complete change of lifestyle, no longer needing to physically be at a place of work in the city. The forced requirement from government to work from home (for those with employment that were able to) was to become the norm. Individuals realising not only did they not need to go into office locations (depending on their type of work) but it suited their lifestyle not to do so or at least not 5 days a week. This led to more property movements out of cities to the countryside within a short space of time.

I'd spent months researching my next purchase, it had to be the right property to get the best return for me. Eventually I had an offer accepted, the purchase process began.

I'd been trying to find a part time job for many months, it was so difficult. It had to fit my still limited abilities, mainly with fatigue and not using the computer too much due to a long-term injury problem with my shoulder and hands. I couldn't quite believe it when after applying for a job at Blenheim Palace, not far from my home, I was asked to an interview. A few days later I was genuinely astonished that they offered me a position as a Palace Guide. It hadn't been made clear until the interview as to how many hours the part time role required. I'd been completely upfront and honest about my health. The position required me to stand for a seven hour shift with a short break at some point, I knew there was no way I could do this. It was very kindly and thoughtfully suggested that five hours would be acceptable, with the prospect to potentially be seated for some of the time. I appreciated that the way their rota worked, they couldn't offer me fewer hours.

  I went for an induction course which was fascinating learning so much about the Palace and behind the scenes that the public never see. Although I loved the experience, I was totally overwhelmed by it, there was so much to learn in a tiny space of time. I had to decide within a few hours as to whether I could accept the job. To my great sadness I realised I didn't have the stamina to do it. I couldn't believe the reply I had to my email declining their offer and thanking them for the wonderful opportunity. It seemed I'd been just the sort of person they needed, they were also sorry that I couldn't take up the role and left it open for me so that if in the future I changed my mind or was able to offer the hours required I just had to let them know. That meant so much to me and I hoped to be able to accept this secondary offer at some point in the future.

It had been quite a stressful few months, I was so looking forward to my planned holiday to my favourite island Menorca. This time I was going with my other best friend Annemarie who I'd known since I was five years old and she six. Two days after arrival I couldn't understand why after a beautiful early evening stroll along the beach chatting happily as we have done all our lives, I was really struggling to walk back to the apartment, I had a strange type of tight pain in my legs and extreme tiredness. The following day a sudden very sore throat led to within hours being confined to bed with what turned out to be Covid.

The confirmed diagnosis of Covid wasn't made until several weeks later. I hadn't, maybe stupidly taken a Covid test kit with me. I spent four days in bed with a fever, persistent cough day and night, streaming nose, muscle aches, complete exhaustion and glands swollen. On my return trips from the bathroom, I tried to spend just a few minutes sitting on the balcony. The row of two-story apartments is located on a protected nature reserve, the edge of a pine forest. Approximately four meters beyond our terrace, an area with shrubbery and grasses. From there the cliff edge dropped three meters to the unbelievably stunning clear turquoise waters. I don't think it's possible to view a more beautiful and alluring sea before my eyes, the waters completely calm and beyond inviting. I had a slight tear in my eyes, I'd travelled so far to enjoy my well-deserved holiday. I was literally so near yet so far from bathing in the most magnificent waters.

To this day I still have no idea how I managed to get home as I was still so unwell, although Annemarie as a highly trained nurse practitioner made the world of difference in aiding me and just being there for me. I truly couldn't have managed without her. There was a point during the first three days that she thought I might have needed to go to hospital if I hadn't shown the slightest indication that I might have been over the worst symptoms before we were due to travel home. The one thing I didn't have to worry about was that Covid restrictions had eased, in that I was allowed to enter the UK without being tested, although I wasn't certain at that time that was the diagnosis, I took every precaution possible on my journey. All testing once home showed a negative result.

The greatest pleasure from my trip was that Annemarie had so deserved a holiday. Working for the NHS during the pandemic had truly tested her as it had all her colleagues in this country. I couldn't recall a time in our very long friendship where I had known her to be under such tremendous, prolonged pressure. For the first time in her lengthy career, I sensed her struggling to cope with a vocation that she'd always been devoted to, at one point describing the workload as 'brutal', so unlike her. She was run ragged physically, mentally, and emotionally not only from the work itself but from scenarios she had witnessed within her healthcare profession.

Between her immense caring for me with her 'never off duty' mode as a nurse even while on holiday, she did manage to have a wonderful time. Having only recently mostly recovered from a nasty period with Covid herself, she was thrilled to improve her health whilst there, the warmth of the sun, daily swimming, snorkelling, sunbathing, reading and a complete change in pace of life, if only for seven days. This is what holidays are meant for.

I expected to feel bad from the exertion of travel when I'd been quite unwell but on returning home, I didn't expect to feel so ill. After nearly three weeks in bed my cough was getting worse, I was given a course of antibiotics which then led to a second course to help clear up a bad chest infection on top of Covid. By the 5th and 6th week it became apparent that as I was starting to feel a fraction better; getting out of bed even just to walk to the bathroom slowly, my pulse was racing, I was out of breath so easily. I tried to walk slowly around my tiny garden just for two or three minutes needing to keep stopping, I was out of breath, tight muscle pains in my legs. My home Pulse Oximeter testing showing intermittent lower levels on any form of tiny exertion. By the 7th week after further consultation from GP's and a couple of visits to my local surgery it was thought that I may have a blood clot in relation to Covid. The John Radcliffe Hospital in Oxford, as with many hospitals all around the country at that time were still trying to cope with large volumes of patients and backlogs so they were unable to see me as an urgent case that afternoon. I was prescribed blood thinning tablets overnight; my friend Sally had stayed with me in order to take me to hospital the next morning for further tests.

Several hours later I was back home. To my huge relief I hadn't had a blood clot but to my complete dismay was given the diagnosis Long Covid. Throughout the two and a half years of the pandemic I had been in absolute fear of getting Covid in case I didn't recover fully, leading to my worst nightmare Long Covid on top of chronic fatigue.

I had to keep on top of this mentally and gave myself firm instructions that I was going to pull through this, and quickly, but my body had other ideas.

CHAPTER THIRTY - FIVE

At the start of June, I completed on my new house purchase. My intention had been to market it as a rental within a few days of returning from holiday, this now had an unforeseen delay. Concerned, I couldn't do anything about it, unaware as to how long the wait might be. Three months later my self-management of the rental process succeeded in finding a suitable tenant very shortly after advertising, they settled in soon afterwards to my huge relief.

By mid-September I had an appointment at the Long Covid clinic at The Churchill hospital in Oxford, it was one of the first areas in the country to set up such clinics, importantly for me within reasonable reach. I also knew there were large numbers of people who needed this clinic, there was a long waiting list. I was so fortunate to be offered a cancellation speeding up my appointment by an estimated several weeks.

I felt so privileged to have a consultation with one of the leading doctors in Long Covid recovery. One of the most profound comments the respiratory consultant said to me was that ...many of the tests that we do on Long Covid sufferers come back as negative or within reasonable boundaries of the norm, but we know there is clearly something wrong so instead of sending you away, (which happened to me for decades with a diagnosis of M.E) we say, we know you are still unwell, what can we do to try and help?

I felt quite moved by this statement, if only this had been the general attitude of many medical staff many years ago with M.E. It wasn't a case they didn't want to help, in most cases they just didn't understand enough, the technology wasn't there to aid in their decision making as to what an earth could they do?

Before I left the Churchill hospital that morning, I had my first appointment with a physio specialising in Long Covid. After about the third week of having Covid when I'd started to feel well enough to get out of bed a little, it was soon apparent that I was struggling with my breathing. It was quite frightening at times, being out of control of your life force is something I've never experienced before, becoming out of breath extremely quickly. At the time of this appointment, it hadn't improved at all. The physio explained to me that over the course of the pandemic it was observed that many people with Covid developed an altered breathing pattern which often accentuated the sensation of breathlessness. A simplified overview can be explained as follows: During the early phase of many illnesses, it's natural for the breathing rate to increase to help fight an infection. Breathing may become shallower which means you breathe using the upper chest and often breathe through the mouth instead of the nose. The bodies response to this stress enhances the process which could make you feel a little panicky, in turn increasing the breathing rate further. If you over-breathe more than your body needs, that can cause tiredness and anxiety resulting in a vicious cycle.

For some patients returning to a normal pattern was all that they needed to begin their journey to recovery, others were more complex. The physio studied my breathing pattern, it was clear I was breathing in this irregular manner.

The session was extremely valuable, such a lovely physio, so understanding and keen to support me. An undeniable relief knowing that someone was actually going to try and help me get through this, I wasn't going to be left on my own. I was signed up to an online workshop with other patients in the same predicament as myself. I was truly so fortunate to have been given this starting point, although it seemed largely because I was so unwell and sent to the John Radcliffe for further assessment in August that I had been offered a place.

Over the next few weeks, the breathing exercises really helped. It needed a lot of focus and attention to retrain my mind in how to breathe normally. It wasn't an easy process and in itself was tiring. I began to make some slow progress, managing a 15 minute walk a couple of times a week, driving a short distance to the nearby town and able to potter in two or three shops before needing to return home. It was clear fatigue was still holding me back. In November

I was signed up to another online workshop, this time an occupational therapist specialising in Long Covid specifically for fatigue.

I'd spent 35 years on an almost daily basis pushing myself through tiredness. This was often unavoidable, completely out of my control. Sometimes because I had no other choice to get through my day, to get things done, to look after my mental health or because I had in my mindset that if I do a little more my body would get used to it, like an athlete in training, therefore gradually improve.

My theory was about to be challenged, in a positive way.

The idea behind the programme was to balance out the parasympathetic nervous system and sympathetic nervous system, they were out of kilter, rather like being in a constant 'fight or flight' scenario. In summary, each activity in the day no matter how small should be stopped before you even began to feel tired, then a period of completely switching off with breathing exercises, mindfulness or similar. Working in this way with the intention to finish the day with no less than 30% of the initial energy the day had started with. Therefore, overtime as the body wasn't over-tiring in the day it should gradually build up a reserve in an 'energy bank' or as I've often referred to, charging a battery.

To begin with you needed to find a baseline, finding a level where no matter what kind of activities were carried out in the day they were achievable without feeling tired. After a few days managing like this, that level should be kept for at least a week, then incrementally increase one thing at a time. As long as caution was taken, doing only what your body was able to without tiring, it should soon become clear if progress was being made, if not reduce the energy usage. This technique had been used successfully with many Long Covid patients.

I found it incredibly difficult to find my baseline, I was warned it could take time to work out. The idea behind it made complete sense and I was really encouraged to think that I could genuinely make considerable progress with the underlying fatigue I'd had for decades as well as Long Covid. This could be a massive breakthrough for me, over time.

Prior to Covid I was 'reasonably' active so if I had known of this programme then, I believe it would have been much easier to work with, slow down my pace, lowering my levels of activity to find a baseline. But now, here I was doing so little it was hard to lessen my daily needs any further for the theory to work. I found it an enormous challenge. I did keep in the back of my mind a couple of important issues. I was determined to be stricter with myself by not pushing through tiredness, that was one of the new instructions I'd been given. Not always easy, of course somethings are often out of your control, but I was going to make a huge effort with this, even if it meant causing problems for other people in some form or another. I matter, and I needed to now come first. Another thing which may seem possibly quite insignificant; After all these years with chronic fatigue I had considered 'rest' as watching TV. After being made clear that this was 'relaxing' not resting, I'd now make this something to adhere to. Resting meant to completely switch off, to be mindful, to literally rest the mind and thoughts. In the past when I was over tired or pushed beyond my limit and needed to go to bed or flop on the sofa, more often than not the first thing I'd do was turn on the TV thinking I was relaxing and resting, now I know better.

I tried various methods that the occupational therapist had suggested to find my baseline, in the end I found my own version. I came up with a system of levels that for me was more positive and productive. Level 1 listing my desired small achievements i.e. talk on the phone for 15 minutes, work on my computer for 15 minutes, walking for a certain number of minutes etc. (I made a separate chart for walking times, starting with five minutes twice a day building up to a thirty minute walk once a day.) Level 2 had small increments from this. For me it seemed a more constructive approach to have specific events and activities to look forward to achieving again, a way to see that I was moving forward.

Earlier in the summer I'd been doing a little research

to see what progress if any was being made with regards to understanding chronic fatigue, potentially finding a cure. I discovered DecodeME, the world's largest study aiming to understand the genetics of why people become ill with ME/CFS, whether the disease is partly genetic and if so try and understand what causes it. It was due to start this year, aiming to get a better understanding of the disease with the hope of eventually finding treatments.

I was so excited by this, a serious move forward in the right direction. During the years that I had been unwell there had been attempts of course to try to understand the illness but so far nothing concrete had come to the fore. As with all research it needs tremendous funding. My understanding is that's been the main cause for decades of delay in finding an answer.

I signed up immediately to see if I could help. They were initially looking for 20,000 volunteers worldwide to provide a saliva sample to study the DNA, an extra 5000 was then added to include people who had developed chronic fatigue after Covid.

I filled out a very lengthy questionnaire, followed a few weeks later with an email to say they had accepted me as part of the research, I'd satisfied their criteria including having had a clinical diagnosis of ME/CFS. A few weeks later a sample test kit arrived in the post, my saliva was hopefully going to help towards a breakthrough. Later in the year I received confirmation that my DNA had been extracted from the sample successfully. I was thrilled, being informed that not everyone who applied would be accepted. There was already evidence from other prior research that there was a genetic part to play in chronic fatigue from 1st, 2nd and 3rd degree relatives.

A brief explanation of the research:

Other studies had looked at biological molecules on patients who were already unwell, but these results might have simply been an effect of the disease rather than the cause.

When we are born our DNA remains unchanged by disease throughout our life, so any DNA difference linked to the disease must be a cause of disease not an effect. Significant differences between the DNA of someone with ME/CFS and healthy controls must therefore reflect the biological cause of the illness.

It wasn't expected to find just one gene revealing the cause but small differences that played a part in the disease leading to a greater understanding. Strong scientific leads with this would mean researchers could continue with new studies with the hope of leading to the development of diagnostic testing and then targeted treatments. Results were expected in 2024. I was highly optimistic but could only keep my fingers crossed.

CHAPTER THIRTY - SIX

In December 2022 my GP's surgery asked me if I would like to take part in some research that Oxford University were carrying out on Long Covid. It involved filling out a very long questionnaire and having blood and urine samples taken.

The study aimed to compare patterns of small molecules in the blood and urine, also looking for differences in molecules relating to the immune system with people suffering with Long Covid, chronic fatigue and other inflammatory conditions. It was hoped it could be understood what might be causing their symptoms. The aim of this research would be to able to find a difference between these conditions, better understand their cause and how future treatments might be improved or developed.

An astonishing piece of information came with the information sheet on the research. It was thought that around the world just over one in five men and nearly one in four women did not get better within the first six weeks after the initial infection from Covid, continuing to suffer symptoms. This figure was quite horrific to me, clearly showing the desperate need to find an answer.

As I was filling out the questionnaire, I suddenly realised for me there was a huge difference between M.E and Long Covid. With M.E or chronic fatigue, I would feel so desperately, deeply fatigued that my body seemed as though every cell had almost completely shut down, using its last scrap of energy just to keep me alive, so much so that there were times when I wanted to take my own life because I couldn't bear the depth of ongoing fatigue and how ill it made me feel. That's how severely the fatigue felt and still could do when I pushed myself to the extreme.

With Long Covid, about six weeks after the initial symptoms, if I sat or lay completely still doing nothing but thinking or looking out the window, I felt absolutely well. It's only when I started to use energy whether reading, talking to someone in person or on the phone, walking or any physical or mental exertion, that's when the symptoms especially fatigue became apparent. It was also becoming clearer that with M.E my body drained of energy more slowly, taking far longer to recover whereas post Covid, fatigue hit me fairly quickly, often within 10 minutes of overdoing an activity, the recovery rate also faster.... until the next time I overdid something, and fatigue caught up with me again.

These were marked differences for me between the two types of fatigue. I could only hope that my tiny involvement in this research might help.

I couldn't believe my bad luck when my next unforeseen delay hit me with full force, literally.

At the end of January 2023, I purchased a new piece of home exercise equipment to encourage myself to increase my fitness. Just prior to my second use I decided to dismount to find my phone so that I could watch an accompanying exercise video whilst on the machine. For some reason I decided to get off backwards whilst turning in readiness to walk away from it. Forgetting momentarily I was a foot higher than ground level, a hard ceramic tiled kitchen floor. I misplaced my step, flew through the air, landing flat on my front with my right arm outstretched in a Superman pose! My shoulder took the brunt of the force, I knew immediately I'd broken something. An hour and a half later at the local minor injuries' unit, an X-ray confirmed I'd fractured my shoulder. I was in shock, literally.

I couldn't believe it, I was just beginning to see the initial signs of progress from Long Covid, my fatigue programme was looking promising and going according to plan, now everything was up in the air again.

Sally was amazing, she came to stay with me for the first three days and nights to help me adjust, begin to learn how to handle my immobility. Her general support and just having someone else in the house allowed me a little time for my body to begin to calm down after the trauma.

Life was once again difficult and for the first 10 days or so very painful. My right arm was nestled tightly in a sling 24/7 with brief episodes unstrapped trying to wash with extreme care, difficulty, immense frustration and daily grumbles with pain. A few minutes twice daily were required for very gentle physio. This was all quite worrying as I had to be so careful not to move a fraction the wrong way with the potential to still need surgery if the fracture moved. Everything about daily life was tricky and exhausting. My neighbours and close friends were brilliant, helping with shopping and small tasks around my home, I couldn't have managed without them.

The next seven and a half weeks were mainly dictated by the importance of physio whilst waiting for a follow up X-ray, delayed because of the then junior doctors strike, hugely disruptive to me and many others.

To my immense relief the bone had healed well, so I'd managed to avoid surgery that I understand isn't particularly successful for my type of fracture. I was discharged from Trauma to continue my long journey with physio that was likely going to take a year.

CHAPTER THIRTY – SEVEN

The next six months seemed to pass so slowly. I couldn't drive for 10 weeks because of my shoulder fracture so this completely interrupted my Long Covid recovery plan, The main thing I could focus on was improving my walking distances, noting I was not only managing to walk further with my graded program but felt fine afterwards, not excessively tired later in the day. I was really pleased with this. Physio by now was taking up quite a lot of time in the day and was also tiring in its own right but I was making slow if good progress with my injury so that was a good thing.

The previous autumn I had booked my usual holiday destination that I loved so much in Menorca, finding it hard at that time to imagine I would be well enough to take a holiday abroad the following year, but I had to be hopeful.

The time had arrived, I felt reasonably confident as I had my best friend Annemarie with me, but I was worried at how much Long Covid would affect my journey and holiday? In the end I managed to enjoy about half my time there, but it was dominated by my fatigue, a huge disappointment to me. I felt quite demoralised as in reality I'd managed more on my first visit there seven years previously when I'd been more consumed with Chronic Fatigue. Long Covid was still weighing me down and I hated it. Due to my lowered level of health, I caught a nasty bug I think, from the flight home despite wearing a mask. The next six weeks were spent recovering from a chest infection setting me backwards yet again on my it seemed, never ending journey to recovery.

For the past twelve months it hadn't been just one illness, injury after another, it was one thing on *top* of the other, why oh why wouldn't life get better for me? I felt I so deserved it.

In October and December I joined webinar sessions held by DecodeME. The outcome of both meetings left me fascinated and excited for the future.

The recruitment to find participants in their genetic study was being ceased in November, the results would be next August 2024. Almost 27,000 questionnaires had been returned, 21,000 saliva sample kits had been sent out. By December 17,000 kits had been returned, so far 15,000 of those had DNA successfully extracted. This was a huge achievement by everyone working at DecodeME and all the participants involved in the study, including myself.

Looking at DNA narrows the scope in being able to find out what's going wrong and therefore easier to move to the next step in the journey to find treatments. The team hoped to find 7 or 8 genes that showed a fault, looking for a strong signal in genetic difference, it should stick out quite clearly. It should give them a clear idea of what system was involved causing the symptoms for chronic fatigue. Was it vascular, mitochondrial, neurological, immunological, a combination of these or something else? From every DNA sample the team were collecting, 1 million chromosomes were being compared to a control DNA sample from a large database.

With a hopeful clear answer, it would then be much easier to partner with experts in whichever field the results directed them to, further research and development potentially finding an answer to help everyone, it might be that they were already available drugs on the market that could help.

From the questionnaire results, two-thirds of the participants had a confirmed viral infection leading to their later diagnosis of chronic fatigue. Whist we all went through the process learning of the horrors of covid, many of us were now fairly familiar with simplified pictures of proteins on our TV screens with the covid virus attacking them. It was a possibility that genetics may have changed proteins in those of us with chronic fatigue therefore changing how an initial virus affected us?

So far, I believe mainly through answers given from the many thousands of questionnaires the DecodeME team had received, it appeared there were different types of M.E and therefore might need different types of treatment. There was already evidence from other prior research that there was a complex genetic part to play in chronic fatigue from 1st, 2nd and 3rd degree relatives.

Someone asked a very logical question during the webinar.

"Why wasn't research being carried out on people who had recovered from M.E?"

"The number of people who recover is very low", came a swift reply from the expert conducting the webinar. This was scary and demoralising to hear but I knew a reality. We were told to be proud of ourselves, this research was a part of history. I held out so much hope a breakthrough would be made, surely it had to after all these years.

CHAPTER THIRTY - EIGHT

Christmas had been an awful time. Some years were easier than others, I could let it gloss over me but this one had been hard, very hard. It's a time of year so many people celebrate, happy to have time off work, enjoy socialising and spending time with their families, for many years this had never been the case for me, it was the hardest day of the year.

Referring back to a previous chapter regarding the core of my inner being that I'm certain I was put on this earth to be a mother, I couldn't accept an invitation if asked to sit around a Christmas table with my immediate relatives (or friends for that matter) because this was their family with their children, I didn't have that.

I just couldn't be there watching and listening to everyone else with their own Christmas traditions they had developed over years with their children, observing the sensation and reality that this was their family that they'd created. I couldn't sit there with a smile on my face pretending to enjoy the atmosphere when the essence of Christmas day is family, particularly children and or grandchildren. In my heart I would be crying, aching, doing my utmost not to let it show externally. The same was true for friends because they were with their children, the bond they had whether they all got along or not was there.

Of course, around the world for many Christmas is not always joyous for entirely different reasons; from war zones to family arguments, missing loved ones who had passed away, maybe one or two important members were missing unable to get to the main gathering, but the core of the theme was always there for me, children, family, I didn't have my own. I am fortunate enough to live in an affluent country where the majority were able to and did celebrate. After many years experiencing this, I'd gone beyond the feeling it was being selfish, it hurt far too much so I did everything to avoid it, staying at home on my own just trying to get through the day, I couldn't be the only one in this position.

2024 started with quite an emotional low that I hadn't experienced to such a depth for quite some years, my walking achievements had become static, some days I was finding it hard to reach the goals that I had set myself. The difference in fatigue between M.E and Long Covid was becoming more apparent to me. The overall fatigue was similar in its abnormality compared to an average healthy person, but I was always more in control of M.E with a slow but steady decline of energy after over exertion with a slow recovery. Long Covid fatigue came almost out of the blue, as though someone had suddenly switched off my engine, unable to restart until adequate rest had been achieved. I felt it controlled me, I became extremely demoralised.

I came across a book by accident 'Forever Strong' by Dr Gabrielle Lyon. It brought me out of the black hole I was well and truly falling into giving me something else entirely different to focus on.

There is much to read on nutrition, but I'd never come across a book that was solely focused on muscles, the vital role they play within our body that I'm almost ashamed to say I had no idea of. If I gave it any thought, in my mind muscles were to protect organs, to give me strength, to hold me together or look aesthetically pleasing. I had absolutely no idea skeletal muscle is the primary engine to extract nutrients, control insulin, regulate cholesterol levels, balance hormones, activate my immune system, and potentially increase survivability from disease. No matter what your age or health history the book illustrated how to potentially overcome everything from obesity to autoimmune disorders and prevent diseases such as Alzheimer's, hypertension, and diabetes. With some scepticism I couldn't put it down, it blew my mind. I found it hard to believe that focusing on having, gaining *healthy* muscle by various means, mainly increasing protein intake balanced with weight and or resistance training could totally transform one's body. A little more complex than that but the general idea behind it.

I implemented its main theory straight away. My diet was actually quite good and healthy, I made a few tweaks, mainly more than doubling my protein intake, it also gave me additional focus on my weight training which I already loved. Within four to six weeks I could see a dramatic difference in my body, this was with only quite minor changes to my diet. After five to six months I'd lost 6 lbs in weight which I could actually do with, menopause flab had caught up with me around my middle even though I'm petite with a small frame it was very noticeable for me. The most astonishing thing I noticed was the change in my body composition even with realistically, a minimal amount of weight training my body shape was changing, looking and feeling stronger with my skin texture smoother and clearer.

The end of July brought the arrival of my sister Sue, it was the start of a seven week family get together with my other New Zealand relatives arriving three weeks later; Dave my brother-in-law whom I hadn't seen for about 15 years and my niece Bex whom I'd seen four years ago. My nephew Alex their son had lived in London for 6 years, he was due to get married at the end of August. I'd been planning how to cope with this event for the previous 18 months since his engagement was announced. The celebrations were to take place 50 miles from me, it was going to be an enormous challenge, but I thought I could somehow manage part of the occasion. I'd been so excited for the event and spending quality time with my relatives. A week after Sue arrived I caught either summer 'flu or another bout of Covid which was going around, I spent the next 10 weeks recovering. There was no hope whatsoever of attending the wedding, I was still in bed at that point coughing my heart out, with immense muscular pain and fatigue feeling very low and demoralised. During Dave and Bex's month long visit only able to spend a few incredibly short periods of time with them. It was all so unfair.

Once again I had to delve very deeply to pull me through yet another huge set back. At the same time my rental property was up for renewal, trying to deal with the self-managerial side of this and finding a new tenant whilst still feeling so unwell was really tough.

Overall, it had been another incredibly challenging year. I'd built up my energy to the level of exercise I had achieved prior to getting the most recent viral infection but somehow my daily life still seemed wasted. I wanted more energy to work even for just a few hours a week, more energy to begin to *live* life, *really live* it, one without so many limitations. I so wanted and needed a partner to share my life with, I wanted to feel joy, freedom, I wanted to smile because I was actually happy not just putting on a brave face the majority of the time masking the true me. I felt so utterly lost in life and alone.

The end of 2024 did bring something new to my life, totally out of the blue. I'd been researching yet again for online work I could do at home. I returned to the only viable option for me, to try and set up my own business with the help of Teemill, a long established online company. It let me construct and start my own business of selling organic clothing. To cut a long story short, I had to build a website from a template they provided, create my own designs, then work at finding customers. They took care of all the customer service. To create this from essentially scratch was quite an achievement, I'd looked at this idea before, but I hadn't had the stamina to proceed with it. Over 6 months I learnt so much, the entire process was all new to me, I can use tech, I learn quite quickly but this was a whole new ball game. During this period, I changed my website in its entirety 6 times, my company name 3 times. A huge learning curve to even begin to understand how to e-commerce works, what to do and how to attract customers. As I write this, half way through 2025, several hundred hours later, I'm starting to see the fruits of my labours, with a few small sales! It's so exciting! We are talking very small numbers, but I have to grow from somewhere. I'm a glass half full person, but if for any reason my business doesn't grow as I would like or hope, the whole process has been immensely important to me and definitely improved my mental strength. Having said that, long may sales continue to rise! It's worked for me because I haven't needed to waste energy travelling to work or deal with the stresses a workplace can bring. I've created this in my own time in as many hours a day as I'm capable of. My proud achievement is called The Organic Runner located at: theorganicrunner.co.uk, please take a look!

2025: Reflecting on time past. For more than 20 years I'd barely been able to leave the house, when I did it was an immense struggle physically and mentally with devastating repercussions. For the next 10 years I had made a little progress but I was still essentially stuck at home the majority of the time pushing myself, almost always resulting in relapses. Or I protected myself because I couldn't bear to continually feel so drained and tired when I tried to do a little more. Here I am 10 years on again I'm approaching my 60th birthday. I have made progress in the last 10 years, yes, but I still live a restricted life. Part of that is because I don't have funding to allow myself to enjoy life much. I haven't been well enough to work for four years I haven't qualified for any benefits for nearly 20 years. I have my income as a landlord but it's a very small property it barely covers essentials let alone extra to start to begin to enjoy my life.

I spent 40 years struggling (is an understatement), pushing through relapses, the cycle repeating itself continually. I don't actually know how I've managed to get this far because this is not the life I envisaged, it still isn't, I've been within seconds of taking my own life on 3 occasions, but thankfully I've literally survived to move forward. I refuse to accept this is how my life must be. I am determined to be well again. I want to live, really live. I deserve to enjoy life, to go on regular holidays, to travel, to go to events, whether near or afar. I deserve to be well enough to spend time with my friends, a whole day with them or better still a weekend, up all day chatting with them like 'well people' do. I deserve to find the love of my life to settle down and get married. I've dreamt of that for more than 50 years. I don't want to be a spinster, that might be an old fashioned term but it hits the mark, it tells you everything, it's a harsh word. I crave to be loved by a husband whom I can share my life with, love him and any family he has. I'm not vain, but I'm a fairly 'OK' looking woman, slender with a heart of gold that's never fully been allowed to be released because I've never had children to devote myself to and love. These descriptions are a part of most people's daily lives across the world, of course it's not contentment every day or every month, but they have the fundamental basis of life, a family; children. They work hard so they deserve to go on holidays, treat themselves. With everything I've been through I more than deserve that. I can't put into words how much I want to begin my life.

Everyone goes through difficult periods in their life I've had 40 years of that, consistently. I haven't *truly* been happy since I was age 20 staying with my sister in New Zealand, standing on a deserted beach staring out to sea, to the world beyond the horizon that I envisaged as fun and exciting and yet to begin. Of course I'm lucky to have the home I have, to be a landlord to have the great long lasting friends and family members I have who will do everything to support me, but they don't live my life they don't live my everyday restricting life the life I live alone. There are always people far worse off than myself, of course, but no one can give me back 40 years of my life.

People around me are retiring, they have pensions to look forward to taking life easy or do things they've always wanted to do whether that means still working part time or finally taking life a little easier than they have been. So many now take this time to travel to spend time with children and grandchildren. That just 'kills me' inside every time I think about it which is most days' because I don't have that. It's *all* I ever wanted it's not much to ask for in life. This may sound as though I'm full of self-pity, well it's true, I am, wouldn't you be reader, if you're honest?

I originally wrote my story for my several reasons:

1. My own benefit, I was literally so seriously unwell I couldn't speak for lengthy periods. I couldn't fully explain to my family or the medical profession just how desperately my body was affected, I had to write it down. For a future me to go back over my traumatic years, to see the immense growth I've achieved in all areas of life.
2. For my family and friends, those closest to me to understand what I was going through enabling them to have some idea how to 'treat me' being so chronically ill.
3. For my future husband who needs to have an understanding of me that can't be easily explained, I feel it needs to be read, to absorb as he reads it.
4. For all of the 100's of thousands of people globally in my position with chronic fatigue or Long Covid. (I'm no medical expert of course but I'm certain these overlap in their core bodily malfunction.) More people understand these days what you mean by these two conditions but many worldwide, as far as I'm concerned still need educating. Even in your most dire seconds and moments of your illness, do everything you can to try and hold on to the glimmer of hope that you won't stay in that utmost of desperate states forever. My torturous pace of

recovery is yes, horrific, but all of our bodies show signs of healing, moving forward as well as backward when they're ready obviously in different ways. I don't believe my epic journey is a standard timeline to base any recovery on. PLEASE, nobody, family, carer or those in the medical profession push us to do more than we are capable.

EPILOGUE THREE

It's time to put my story to bed.

I'm not yet where I want to be, but look how far I've come, being bed bound to being out of bed all day, walking, weight training, running my own online business and being a landlord. Going abroad for short holidays, I'm planning a helicopter ride for an upcoming 'big' birthday, the one that has a zero on the end! I'm also contemplating studying for a potential new role as a part time personal trainer? Emotionally I've still yet to find stability in a long term relationship, it's remains an enormous gap in my life.

My 60th birthday is looming. I will never be able to let go of everything I've been through, I will always feel I've been cheated, having had almost 4 decades of my life taken away from me, having a disease that's totally controlled me. But, it's made me who I am today, I can't do anything but accept that, I can't get those years back.

At the start of my story, I said, …'this is not the life I would have chosen', of course it's not, but it's the life I've been through, it's a life that in some respects has carried on without me. Envy and jealousy still play a role in my thoughts. The majority of people in the western world take so much for granted, the simplest of things in life, they're all that I ever wanted, a normal everyday life.

Since Long Covid first became a major global health issue, research into this terrible debilitating condition alongside its partner in crime; chronic fatigue, is moving forward, in turn aiding a potential cure for M.E. I believe there HAS to be an answer; it WILL be found. I WILL do everything in my willpower to be able to see that day in my lifetime, so that I can once again experience what it feels like to be well. This passion still drives me, I REFUSE to give up. Chronic fatigue will NOT get the better of me, I will NOT let it totally consume the rest of my life.

I still have too much strength in me to give up. I deserve and have in my mind and heart to LIVE my life, to be out there, to meet my husband, to travel the world. Apart from 2 lengthy trips to New Zealand prior to chronic fatigue, I've never had a 2 week holiday, I long for that. I deserve to earn money to treat myself even with small luxury's, just everyday life indulgences that not many people view as luxurious. I ask the universe' to please bring these things to me, I will be the **most grateful** person there ever could be.

ABOUT THE AUTHOR

Katie was born and raised in West Oxfordshire, educated in Oxford. She continues to live in this beautiful part of the country loving the tranquillity of rural life, happiest when walking in the surrounding fields absorbing the sights and sounds.

She is finally beginning to enjoy living a life that she spent too many years missing out on.

There are two great sadness's in Katie's life. Firstly, chronic fatigue has cruelly stripped her of the opportunity to become a mother and secondly, she so wishes her mum and dad Isobel and Craig could see how well she is today, she sometimes 'feels' them looking down on her smiling.

UNVEILING VITALITY A New Life Emerging From Chronic Fatigue

Printed in Dunstable, United Kingdom